Larry Lachman, Psy.D.
Diane Grindol
Frank Kocher, D.V.M.

A FIRESIDE BOOK *Published by Simon & Schuster*
New York London Toronto Sydney Singapore

Birds

OFF THE

Perch

THERAPY AND TRAINING
for Your Pet Bird

FIRESIDE
Rockefeller Center
1230 Avenue of the Americas
New York, NY 10020

For information regarding special discounts for bulk purchases,
please contact Simon & Schuster Special Sales at
1-800-456-6798 or business@simonandschuster.com

Photographs throughout © 2003 Diane Grindol

Designed by Bonni-Leon Berman

Manufactured in the United States of America
10   9   8   7   6   5   4   3   2

Library of Congress Cataloging-in-Publication Data
Lachman, Larry.
    Birds off the perch : therapy and training for your pet bird /
[Larry Lachman, Diane Grindol, Frank Kocher].
        p.   cm.
    Includes bibliographical references (p. 197–200).
    1. Cage birds—Behavior.   2. Cage birds—Training.
I. Grindol, Diane.   II. Kocher, Frank.   III. Title.
SF461.6 .L33   2003
636.6'8—dc21   2002036661

ISBN 0-7432-2704-2

To "Calicio," the cardinal whom I would listen and whistle
to when walking home from grade school.
This book is for you and your "flock."
—*Larry Lachman, Psy.D.*

To the dedicated souls who place our bird companions
in new homes when they need them, and to those
who educate people about companion bird care and
behavior to ensure that our avian companions are well
cared for and cherished by their families.
—*Diane Grindol*

To Kathryn Kocher.
—*Frank Kocher, D.V.M.*

In memory of ornithologist Dr. Luis F. Baptista,
Curator of Birds, California Academy of Sciences.

Acknowledgments

No ideas, including our own, arise from a vacuum. Although we are solely responsible for the ideas and techniques outlined in this book, there have been many outstanding psychologists and animal behaviorists, and many great friends, who have had a profound impact on us and our way of thinking about pet bird behavior.

Dr. Frank wishes to thank the dedicated researchers and veterinarians of the Veterinary Information Network, such as Dr. Brian Speer, for providing critical information for his chapters on veterinary care and treatment. He also wishes to acknowledge Richard D. Macy, D.V.M., George Nolan Thomas, D.V.M., and Duane Hauser, D.V.M., for introducing him to the practice of veterinary medicine. In addition, Dr. Frank would like to thank Karen Fenstermaker, D.V.M., Amanda Sharp, D.V.M., Molly Williams, D.V.M., Kristen Lawmaster, D.V.M., and Bonnie Burns, D.V.M., who have worked with him and assisted him in making time to write this book. Thanks also go to Todd Lawmaster, D.V.M., for reviewing manuscripts, and Mike Murray, D.V.M., for veterinary medical advice on many cases. Finally, Dr. Frank would like to thank the former and current staff of the Ocean View Veterinary Hospital for their continued support for this project as well as many others.

In the companion bird arena, Diane would like to acknowledge the dedicated parrot behavioral consultants who have paved the way toward living in harmony with these complex birds. Diane thanks Chris Davis and Sally Blanchard especially for their years of writing and lectures about parrot behavior. She furthermore thanks Liz Wilson, Phoebe Greene Linden, Mattie Sue Athan and Pamela Clark for their insights. Diane remembers with fondness Dr. Luis Baptista (to whom this book is dedicated), who contributed to her understanding of bird behavior through his research and inquiring mind. Diane acknowledges the inspiring research of Dr. Irene Pepperberg, and the ongoing parrot behavior research of the Psittacine Research Project at UC Davis, including that by director Dr. James Millam, researcher Dr. Cheryl Meehan and student Rebecca Fox, M.S.

Diane would also like to thank personal friends and bird-sitters who made it possible for her to work on this book. These include Judy Murphy and her yellow-naped Amazon, Cisco, Bev Owens and her flock, including Toby the cockatiel, Doris and Ron Wilmoth, and Tawny Williams. Diane's life interest in birds was immeasurably influenced by Dr. Michael Murray, D.V.M., and Tom Roudybush, M.S. She would also like to acknowledge the encouragement and support of Fancy Publications editors throughout the years that she has contributed to *Bird Talk* magazine. Melissa Kauffman, in particular, has been a steady support in her positions with regard to bird-related material from Fancy Publications.

In the human-behavior arena, Dr. Larry would like to acknowledge Dr. Salvador Minuchin, Dr. Aaron Beck, Dr. Albert Ellis and the two great pioneers in behaviorism, Dr. Joseph Wolpe and Dr. B. F. Skinner. In the animal-behavior arena, Dr. Larry would like to acknowledge the influences of William Campbell, Dr. Ian Dunbar, Dr. Stanley Coren, the Carmel/Salinas-based "fearsome-fivesome"—Andee Burleigh, Suzie O'Brien, Suzie Bluford, Barbara DeGroodt and Pat Miller, as well as Diana Guerrero, Lori Agon, Sherri Regalbuto, Jodi Andersen and Karen Pryor.

In addition, the authors would like to thank the following people who had an unwavering belief in this project from its inception: Sue Marino, Suzanne Mulcahy, James Brull, Nashoma

Carlson, Dr. Marty Becker, Arden Moore, Kate Colby, Gabriella Graham, Julia Hutton, Randy and Judy Stein, Maria Tello, Susan Schustak, Gary Zager, Kathy "Kat" Albrecht, Dr. Pete Keesling, Steve Dale, Bob Vella, Joe Bauer and Karen Yamada.

Finally, we must recognize our editors at Simon & Schuster, Lisa Considine and Anne Bartholomew, for their professionalism, support and enthusiasm for *Birds off the Perch*. Dr. Larry and Dr. Frank want to acknowledge what an outstanding job Diane Grindol did as photographer for this book. Finally, Dr. Larry, Diane and Dr. Frank would like to thank their parents, their partners and/or their children for being there when it counted.

—*Larry Lachman*
—*Diane Grindol*
—*Frank Kocher*

Contents

Contents
xiv

part three
Ornithology and the Olympics

Introduction

Even before Dr. Larry's second book, *Cats on the Counter: Therapy and Training for Your Cat,* was published, people who knew he was writing it already were asking: When was he going to do one on birds? Who would have thought birds, too, needed behavior therapy?

But pet birds are no less prone to behavior problems than cats or dogs. There are now 15 million pet birds in the United States (with ornithologists recognizing nearly 9,000 species of birds compared to 4,400 species of mammals). Pet bird sales have literally skyrocketed over the last few years. Macaws, Amazons, budgies, parrots, cockatoos, cockatiels, finches—it seems there's a burgeoning market for birds of every type! Given the fact that 60.8 percent of bird-owning households are "parent-based"— consisting of young couples or parents under the age of forty-five with children under the age of six—conflicts within the family system between owner and bird, or child and bird, are common.

The behavior problems that Dr. Larry, Diane, and Dr. Frank most frequently encounter in pet birds are biting, screaming and feather plucking. These bird behavior problems are most common in young birds, and when you consider that most pet-bird-owning households have a bird that is under six years of age, it's easy to see why so many people have expressed a need for this book.

We focus this book on the *five* areas that encompass about 99 percent of behavior problems in birds:

- biting or aggression toward the owner
- screaming
- sibling bird rivalry
- jealousy toward the human members of the "flock"
- feather plucking

What is most critical in treating these behaviors successfully is for each member of the family to communicate with your bird consistently—this is what Dr. Larry calls *structural family therapy.* Positive reinforcement, refraining from accidentally rewarding inappropriate behavior, encouraging healthy behavior, and practicing nonviolent training are all key components of raising a happy, healthy pet bird.

Throughout this book, you'll read short case histories from Diane's, Dr. Frank's and Dr. Larry's files, detailing what they or their colleagues did to help treat a particular bird for its behavior problem.

Beyond the behavior therapy aspect of this book, you'll also find entertaining and important information on how to match your personality with the right pet bird, complete sections on veterinary care your bird needs, and methods of training your bird to talk, dance or even play basketball! You'll find that birds are *more* of a challenge to train than dogs, but *less* of a challenge to train than cats. This is because, as members of a flock, birds share a dog's "pack" mentality. At the same time, birds are not as dependent on their people as dogs are because, like horses, birds are *prey* animals. The treatment plan for a dog with a specific behavior problem often requires several modifications along the way, but usually takes just four to eight weeks to successfully implement. The treatment plan for a cat usually requires *less* tweaking and is more straightforward, but because the cat is not as socially dependent on its person, it usually takes about sixteen to twenty-four weeks to bring about a cure. Birds are in the middle: behavior programs require less tweaking than with the codependent dog, but they may take longer to effect a cure, usually between eight to sixteen weeks. Don't be dismayed—some bird species can live more than *sixty years!* Establishing good behavior at the start means you and your pet bird may enjoy a long, happy life together.

The number-one reason we write books on pet therapy and care is to cut down on the number of pets either being given away, abused or euthanized because their owners believed that they couldn't make them behave. As Dr. Larry likes to say, by learning more about your pet, you will also end up learning more about yourself. It is our hope that this book guides and enlightens you as you welcome your pet bird into its new "flock."

—*Larry Lachman, Psy.D., Carmel, California*
—*Diane Grindol, Monterey, California*
—*Frank Kocher, D.V.M., Pacific Grove, California*
September 2002

part one

Choosing and Caring FOR A Pet Bird

CHAPTER 1

Birds of a Feather Fly Together

Picking the Right Bird for You

*So live that you wouldn't be ashamed to sell
the family parrot to the town gossip.*
—WILL ROGERS

So you're thinking of getting a companion bird? Or you're adding
to your flock? It makes a difference in your happiness if you are
living with a species of bird *compatible with your lifestyle and personality.* In addition to examining the family system, you should
also consider your individual personality type and your pet bird's
natural temperament. But a word of warning before we do this:
Any individual bird may differ from the temperament generaliza-

tions customarily assigned to its species as a group. The following descriptions that we provide are merely to serve as pointers, a place to start if you are considering what kind of bird to get.

Matching Your Personality with the Right Bird

In both of his earlier books, *Dogs on the Couch* and *Cats on the Counter,* Dr. Larry emphasized the importance of matching your personality style with the right breed of dog or cat. The same applies to selecting the bird species best suited for you and your family.

Dr. Larry uses the concepts of "personality types" developed by analytic psychologist Dr. Carl Jung, who once served as a protégé of Sigmund Freud, along with two personality tests designed to assess these personality types: the Myers-Briggs Type Indicator and the Keirsey Temperament Sorter Test. Using these concepts and tests, Dr. Larry describes four "base" temperament types for people. You can be an "SP" type (Sensation/Perceiving), who needs to be free to act on impulse and yearns for action and fun. You can be an "SJ" type (Sensation/Judging), who needs to be useful to society, to belong and be appreciated by your social group for doing hard work. You can be an "NT" type (Intuitive/Thinking), who needs to be in control, likes organization, and seeks competence. Or you can be an "NF" type (Intuitive/Feeling), who needs to be in the moment, to be authentic, and has to "feel" things out first. By taking either the Myers-Briggs or the Keirsey Temperament Sorter (www.keirsey.com), you can come up with your "base" type and then know what personality temperament you are and match the right species of bird to that temperament style.

In addition, some species of pet birds *also* demonstrate SP, SJ, NT or NF–like characteristics (see the following chapter for more details). Assessing *both* your own personality temperament and the temperament of your prospective pet bird is an important *pre-*

ventive measure against ending up with a severe mismatch, which can lead to a serious behavior problem and/or having to adopt out your fine feathered friend.

The Most Popular Companion Bird

Despite the allure of the largest parrots, in reality it is a few species of small birds that are most commonly kept as pets in the U.S. These include cockatiels, budgies, lovebirds, canaries, zebra finches and doves. Cockatiels, the "NFs" of the bird world, are small, crested parrots originally native to Australia. They are related to the much larger cockatoos and have characteristics that many people look for in a companion parrot. Cockatiels deserve their popularity. They like to be held and scratched, and are extremely interactive with their owners. Cockatiels stay tame and friendly throughout their lives, with a life expectancy as long as twenty-five years. Cockatiels make good companions for people of many ages. They can entertain themselves when they belong to a person who works outside the home, they are generally gentle enough for responsible children to handle, and they are outstanding companions to both students and the elderly. Cockatiels have been in captivity for about 150 years, long enough to develop many pleasing color mutations. They are also a small bird, with a smaller price tag than many parrot species, and space requirements that can be met by most households.

Budgerigars, popularly known as "budgies," the "SPs" among pet birds, are often considered children's pets. They blossom under the tutelage of an adult, so don't discount the satisfaction available from working with a gregarious budgie. Male budgies can develop the largest vocabularies of any parrot species. One budgie mentioned in the *Guinness Book of Records* acquired a vocabulary of more than 1,700 words by the time he was four years old. Budgies vocalize in a fast, high-pitched voice. It's not uncommon for someone to have a talking budgie without knowing it. Be alert to your budgie's vocalizations! Budgies come in a fantastic variety of colors and color combinations. Generally, males are friendlier than females when kept as pets. Budgies don't like to sit and be petted or cuddled, but will learn to perch readily on a finger and to accept other restraint and handling. Budgies like to be with their human companion and can be trained to stay on a play perch or shoulder as you go about activities. Budgies can live ten to twelve years, though many die by the time they are four years old. Budgies are prone to cancer, and that has shortened their life expectancy.

Lovebirds have a pugnacious personality. Lovebirds make good companion birds if obtained as a hand-fed baby, then handled on a regular basis. They love to tunnel and burrow into things, like pockets or T-shirts. Female peach-faced lovebirds have an endearing habit of tucking sticks or leaves into their rump feathers to use to make nests. There are three species of lovebirds commonly available, with many mutation colors in each species: peach-faced lovebirds, Fischer's lovebirds, and masked lovebirds. The peach-faced lovebirds are most often kept as pets. Despite their reputation, you shouldn't keep lovebirds with others of their own or different species. They can be nasty cage mates for another bird, but loving individual people companions.

Canaries, finches, and doves are quiet, hands-off pets. They should be provided with an enclosure with room to fly and a proper diet for their species, but they don't require the same amount of socialization as many parrot species. Canaries have been in captivity for about 500 years. There actually are "breeds" of canaries. You shouldn't expect that every canary will be a yellow Tweety bird. Canaries come in colors from sparrow brown to bright red, and with types from trim singers to elongated living feather dusters. If you want a singing canary, you will want to choose a male and keep him by himself. Usually the best time of year to find a canary is in the fall, when breeders are picking out which youngsters to keep for the next year and which need to find new homes. Canaries actually learn new songs every spring, so offer your male canary plenty of music and birdsong.

There are many types and colors of finches, with price tags that also vary. Do your homework about the finch species you choose to keep. Some need live food in their diet, or commonly lay their eggs in another species' nest and so should be housed with a separate species. The type of nest or sleeping quarters they require will vary, so you should learn all you can before setting up a cage of finches. Most finches are kept in pairs or colonies. Both zebra finches and society finches are common, hardy species.

Doves or pigeons have much to recommend them as gentle pets. They don't bite and they do make a lovely "cooing" sound. Most often, doves are kept in aviaries, but small diamond doves or a single ring-necked dove could be kept in a cage and socialized as a pet. There are myriad dove and pigeon breeds. Some tumble in the sky, homing pigeons are trained to race long distances, and there are pigeons with outlandish coloring and feathering.

What Did You Say?

People are drawn to birds because of their ability to use our language. Though most parrot species have the potential for learning to speak, some are more likely to pick up human language.

The bird species most likely to talk include the African grey parrot (the "NTs" of the parrot world), Timneh African grey, yellow-naped Amazon, double yellow-headed Amazon, eclectus parrots (the "SJs" of the bird world), blue and gold macaw (one of the "SP" temperament species of the bird world), lories, ring-necked parakeets and some conures (also "SPs" of the bird world). A few non-parrot species are also good talkers. These include the mynah, crow and starling.

With somber grey feathers, a prominent patch of white facial skin and a flash of bright red only in their tail feathers, African grey parrots and Timneh African grey parrots are not highly colored. They are renowned, however, for their ability to accurately mimic sounds and voices. An African grey parrot not only learns words and phrases, but can learn to imitate different voices. Occasionally, a companion grey may not learn to talk at all. Our high expectations for greys come from the results of intelligence research by Dr. Irene Pepperberg with Alex the African grey. Alex has learned to name the shape and material of objects, as well as to voice comparisons such as same and different. As a companion, African greys are not always cuddly, but they are intelligent and companionable. Their natural calls are clicks and whistles, which earn a grey the label of a "quiet" parrot. Of course, if a grey learns a cockatiel call or even a canary trill, it will come out at a big grey-sized volume and you'll rethink the "quiet" designation.

An African grey parrot or Timneh can live for fifty years, perhaps more. The grey is an intelligent and sensitive species. They need intellectual stimulation and companionship. A grey who does not receive socialization and stimulation may well turn to feather-plucking out of boredom or anxiety. Greys are susceptible to Psittacine Beak and Feather Disease, especially in the first three years of his life. Talk to your veterinarian about prevention of this fatal disease in your pet. Both male and female African grey parrots can talk and can be good companion birds. These birds do not have external signs of their sex; to know a male from a female will require a DNA blood test or surgical sexing.

Many of the large Amazon species speak clearly. Yellow-naped and double yellow-headed Amazon parrots are every pirate's fantasy bird. They are stocky, short-tailed, predominantly green birds. They often have large, loud and hilarious vocabularies. The double yellow-headed Amazon gains a yellow head as it matures, with markings varying widely among individuals. The yellow-naped Amazon is an even larger bird, usually with a tick of yellow at the back of the neck.

Amazons are not dependent on their human companions. They're independent and capable of entertaining themselves. Both sexes of these species are talented talkers, because they are naturally verbal birds. In fact, these are large birds with large voices. Keep that in mind in case you're considering an Amazon. Amazon parrots have gained a reputation as nippy birds that bite without warning. Those who know them best learn to read their body language, and also learn not to try to handle an excited Amazon. Some warning signals are flashing eyes or a wide-spread tail and stiff movements. Setting strict limits for your Amazon is also helpful. These birds are intelligent and need guidance.

Since our companion birds cannot be neutered, most do exhibit some sexual behavior. Amazon parrots are famous for being "hormonal" in the spring, and it is at that time they are particularly difficult to handle. They are also vocal in these seasonal periods. These episodes are most severe when the bird is five to twelve years old. Hang in there, and you'll have many calmer years with a bird who will live to be fifty or more years old. Because of the discipline required to work with an Amazon parrot, and the subtlety involved in reading their "I'm gonna bite" behavior, this is not a good species to choose for families with children.

Both species are among the commonly smuggled species, as they come to us from Central and South America as well as Mexico. Buy your yellow-naped or double yellow-headed Amazon from a reputable breeder. If one of these Amazons is offered to you at a price that's too low to believe, look elsewhere. It is not worth supporting bird smuggling and the parrot abuse associated with it.

Eclectus parrots can be incredibly talented talkers. The male birds are predominantly green, and the females are predominantly red. They make striking couples. Since the sex of most parrots is not evident, this is a plus for the eclectus and makes naming them easier. Eclectus are low-key, quiet parrots. Both sexes can talk, though there is no guarantee that that an eclectus will talk. Eclectus who do talk are adept at learning words, phrases and songs, and speak almost as clearly as an African grey parrot. An eclectus doesn't demand a lot of an owner's attention to be happy, a positive characteristic in busy homes. There are four species of eclectus parrots available in the U.S. They vary somewhat in coloration and size, but are kept equally well as companion birds. All of the eclectus are large parrots and require an appropriately sized cage and play area, along with a supply of chewable toys, and interesting toys and experiences to stimulate their intellect. Eclectus are bright birds, but that's not always a person's first impression. They are deliberate in their movements. When you ask an eclectus to step "up" on your hand, he will think about it for a while, then slowly react. This is not a bird for an impatient owner. Eclectus have bright, iridescent feathering that is almost fur-like and they need to bathe frequently. An eclectus owner should discuss their diet thoroughly with an eclectus expert before taking on their care and feeding. They don't respond to formulated diets as well as other parrots, and will need a lot of fresh foods in their diet.

Lories are bright, brightly colored and intelligent companion parrots. They have special dietary and caging needs, as most species of lories eat nectar and fruit, thus producing loose squirts for droppings. Likewise, softbill talkers such as the mynah, crow and starling have special dietary and caging needs appropriate to the species. It is illegal to keep our native crows as pet birds, but there are non-native species that can be kept and trained to talk. Starlings live in the wild in the U.S., but are an introduced species and so can be brought up as a cage bird and trained to talk.

The ring-necked parakeet and many talking conure species, such as the blue-crowned conure, are affordable for more people than larger parrots. Like most parakeets, the ring-necked parakeet is not cuddly or affectionate as a pet, but can learn to speak very clearly. Talkative birds are verbal birds, so keep in mind that none of these species are recommended for the urban or apartment dweller.

Velcro Birds Love Cuddling

Many a companion bird owner has been smitten by the loving, cuddly quality of an umbrella cockatoo. These, along with another large white cockatoo, the Moluccan (the "NFs" of the bird world), are also those most frequently turned in to parrot adoption and rescue centers. If you're at all interested in a cockatoo, do a lot of reading about the species and learn how to acclimate your bird to living with your family. Learn about avian adolescence, so that you can get through it with your companion without adding to parrot rescue statistics.

Umbrella cockatoos are large white cockatoos with an impressive crest, which they can raise when startled or alarmed. The underside of their wings and tail is lemon yellow. They can raise most of the feathers on their body, and will do so in an aggressive stance, or if you design a dancing play activity with one. Cockatoos like to posture when they play, making wild head and wing movements, bouncing and pacing and acting crazy. They're good companions for actors and dancers. Like all of the cockatoos, including cockatiels, umbrella cockatoos produce down feathers that disintegrate into powder. If you have allergies or respiratory problems, this is not the bird for you. Umbrella cockatoos can live to be eighty years old. There is a commitment involved in obtaining an umbrella cockatoo who needs to be provided for past your own lifetime. Umbrella cockatoos are indeed cuddlers, accepting endless amounts of cuddling and handling. Most people don't have endless amounts of time to spend doing this, so an umbrella cockatoo should also be taught to entertain herself.

The Moluccan is a majestic cockatoo. The Moluccan is large and white. If fed a diet high in vitamin A, a Moluccan approaches a light peach in coloration. Their crest is salmon-colored and can be lifted in an impressive display. Occasionally, a Moluccan will learn to speak in a small, soft voice. Male cockatoos can become vocal, aggressive and demanding as they reach maturity. They are one of the parrots most frequently turned in to adoption centers.

In breeding situations, aggressive males may injure their mates, so some arrive via this route as well. The sad thing is that the Moluccan cockatoo is an endangered species. We should think carefully about how we are managing our important population of these parrots. A Moluccan cockatoo may live to be eighty or older. They are more sensitive and more demanding than an umbrella cockatoo. They're larger birds as well. A Moluccan cockatoo may feather pick after changes in a household. They are susceptible to Psittacine Beak and Feather Disease (PBFD). Moluccans can develop incessant screaming behaviors. Their larger frame produces louder vocalizations than those of an umbrella cockatoo. This is not the bird for everyone. They need behavioral guidance, a prudent amount of cuddling and a great understanding of cockatoo behavior.

Cockatoos are high-strung, sensitive and manipulative birds. A cockatoo naturally has morning and evening periods of boisterous glad-to-be-alive screaming. This is at a decibel level that can rattle walls and numb eardrums. You do not want to raise a cockatoo who becomes a problem screamer. Cockatoos can be picky eaters. If you're searching for a young cockatoo, find one that has been weaned to a variety of foods and continue to offer your companion a banquet of foods. Cockatoos are notorious for developing feather-picking and screaming behavior problems. They are susceptible to the fatal Psittacine Beak and Feather Disease, so you should talk to your veterinarian about testing for and preventing this disease in your companion bird.

Pint-Sized Birds

Parrots come in all shapes and sizes. Senegals, Meyer's and brown-headed parrots are small but colorful, and quiet enough to live in an apartment. Parrotlets are the size of a thumb. Green-cheeked conures delight many owners.

The Senegals, Meyer's and brown-headed parrots are from the

family of small African parrots called the *poicephalus*. Senegals are the best known and most widely available members of their family. Hand-fed Senegal parrots make outstanding parrot companions. They are small-sized compact parrots with short tails. Senegals are mostly green, with grey heads and improbably bright yellow or orange markings on their chest that make them look like they're dressed in fashionable vests. Though a Senegal, Meyer's or brown-headed parrot, like any parrot, can have behavioral screaming problems, they most often use soft vocalizations. Occasionally a Senegal parrot will learn to talk in a squeaky mechanical voice and they can be taught trick behaviors as well. The Senegal is a suitable choice for an apartment parrot. All parrots go through a sort of "teething" stage just after they wean. Parrots don't have teeth, so they don't teethe. Just after weaning, however, they nibble on everything. They test the boundaries of teething on human fingers, furniture and all types of food. The Senegal especially needs consistent, gentle behavior training at this stage. Then you'll have a wonderful companion for thirty or more years to come.

Parrotlets are feisty and don't know that they're the size of Tom Thumb. As diminutive parrots, they are easy to house. Expect to spend plenty of time working with that big parrot personality though!

Many conures are loud and gregarious, but a few are smaller, quieter birds such as the green-cheeked conure. These cockatiel-sized birds are little clowns like their cousins and are attractively marked. They like being in pockets, will play on their backs and can learn to speak.

Breathtaking Birds

One of the things that attracts people to birds is their striking coloration. Some outstanding examples in the bird world include the sun conure, the large macaws, such as the blue and gold macaw, scarlet macaw and green-winged macaw, eclectus parrots and the lories.

The sun conure is a gorgeous bird with a loud, raucous call. Anyone who sees an adult sun conure for the first time finds it hard to forget this bright yellow bird with orange trim and green wing feathers. Anyone who is seriously considering sharing their abode with a sun conure should spend some time listening to the vocalizations this species can produce. They have a strident call. This is an appropriate bird for a family who has no close neighbors, those with deaf neighbors and those who love their bird so much they can overlook its call. A sun conure is a medium-sized bird with a long tail. They're playful and will enjoy being handled. Conures love to be placed on their back and love to crawl in things. Conures have a sense of humor and affection for their owner. The conures and macaws are probably closely related species, with similar personality traits. If you are attracted to the gaudily colorful but much larger macaws, a conure is a good choice. A conure companion will share your life for up to forty years. They are not demanding birds. A conure will entertain himself while you're at work. He'll like some scratches and affection, and plenty of play, but will usually not become neurotic about changes in his environment.

The blue and gold macaw is a stunning clown of a bird who may also talk well. The blue and gold macaw is a striking bird, with iridescent turquoise feathers and a bright gold chest. You can probably guess that this huge macaw has a huge voice. If you choose to have a macaw in your life, everything about keeping him will be huge. Can you provide a bird with a five-foot wingspan adequate space to exercise? A macaw nibbles on trees for entertainment. Can you provide adequate material for that? Take time to learn about macaws before you invest in one. They are adapted to a low protein, high fat diet and their care requires the purchase of large quantities of nuts. Yes, this is the kind of bird who can crack a Brazil nut with his beak.

The green-winged macaw is a very large bird and quite gentle, though not widely available. The green-winged macaw is deep red, with a light colored upper beak and distinct feathers on its area of facial skin. The scarlet macaw has a reputation for being nippy as a companion parrot, but is indescribably beautiful. It is bright red, with a band of yellow on its wings and no apparent feathers on its bare facial patch. The hyacinth macaw is very endangered in the wild. It is the largest of the macaws, with the loudest voice. Hyacinths are known as the "gentle giants" for their even temperaments. Macaws are intelligent, interesting companions, but socializing them at a young age is important. A macaw loves to play and wrestle. They have a sense of humor, and the blue and gold macaw can often talk quite well. A macaw's normal method of testing a new acquaintance and at times his owner is called "bluffing." The bird comes rushing at the person, formidable beak extended and threatening to bite. This is bluffing because the macaw doesn't intend to bite at all. It is quite a show, however. If a person gives way, the macaw loves to play the game over and over. As a macaw owner, you'll have to learn to work with this behavior and to establish good behavior guidelines while your bird is young. Macaws become sexually mature at about five years of age and can live to be seventy-five years old. A macaw is a large, long-term investment and should be considered carefully. This is not the right bird for most home situations.

Long-Lived Birds

Some of the longer living birds include the large cockatoos and large macaws. Zoos have documented cockatoos that have lived into their eighties. A Moluccan cockatoo at the San Diego Zoo was at least eighty years old when he died. Since he had been caught in the wild, his exact age was unknown. A Leadbeater's cockatoo at Chicago's Brookfield Zoo is the only animal left from their original collection—he's now in his sixties. Macaws have a prospective lifespan of seventy-five years, and the Amazons live to their forties and fifties. With the longevity of parrots comes the responsibility of providing for your companion beyond your own death. If you have a long-lived species of parrot as a companion, consider ensuring that the bird makes friends among your acquaintances, and that it is clear to your friends and family where your bird should go when you can no longer care for him.

Though the cockatoos, macaws and Amazons can be long-lived, they may also succumb at earlier-than-expected ages to many ailments. These include ailments linked to obesity and stress as well as household accidents.

The Secret Pet Bird

There are many species of birds that are not common companion birds, but which make excellent pets. It's too bad they aren't more popular. Though little known as companions, parrots of the pionus species have a lot to recommend them. They are medium-sized parrots who are sturdily built like an Amazon, but have very quiet, mellow personalities. All of the pionus have a prominent eye ring and a triangular patch of red feathers under their tails. The Maximillian pionus can be a good talker, while the smaller bronze-winged and blue-headed pionus are more subdued companions. Two Amazon species to consider as steady, happy family companions are the orange-winged and the lilac-crowned Amazons. They are medium-sized parrots with even temperaments. The Timneh grey is just as talented at talking as his bigger cousin, the Congo African grey. A Timneh's top beak is horn-colored and his tail is maroon instead of the bright red of a Congo's tail. If cockatoos are attractive to you but you'd like a parrot who is lower maintenance than an umbrella or Moluccan cockatoo, consider the small Goffin's cockatoo. Goffin's are lively companions that fit into many families.

If you're considering a conure, meet a few blue-crowned conures. They're often personable, talkative birds. Though not the stunning sunny yellow of the sun conure, they are still attractive and their decibel level is slightly (I said slightly) lower. In fact, if you're thinking that a macaw should join your family, you'll find the same personality in a conure or a mini macaw, without the necessity to build a rain-forest habitat on your property. The mini macaws include the yellow-collared macaw and severe macaw as well as the diminutive, conure-sized Hahn's macaw. As you read about the socialization characteristics of parrots, as well as their vocal abilities, are you a little intimidated? Hands-off birds such as canaries or finches can provide you with companionship. Their care is different from that of parrots. Be sure to learn how to care for the species you choose. Finally, if you can't stand the thought of *ever* being bitten by your companion animal, consider a dove as a companion bird!

Bringing Birdie Home: Things to Prepare

Once you've made that all-important decision about what species of bird to adopt, you'll want to make your new bird's arrival as smooth as possible. Bringing a playful, passionate bird into your family will cause disruption as well as excitement (affecting the entire family system, as described earlier). Your bird will look like an adult, even if he is a youngster. He will have attained his full size and feathering before he comes to your house. His mannerisms will still be those of a baby, however, and he'll still be learning things.

If you bring an older bird into your home, he will be adjusting to a new "flock" at your house and will start learning your flock's language and schedule. If he's learned manipulative behaviors, he may try those out with your family. Here are some things to keep in mind:

- **Education first.** Learn all you can about your new bird from his breeder, the pet store where you find him, or his former family. Your first concern in moving your bird to join your

The 411 of Popular Pet Birds

Bird Species	Loudness	Size	Talking Ability	Energy Level	Lifespan	Cuddly Quotient	Independence	Apartment Candidate
African grey parrot	Medium: vocalizations are clicks, whistles and talking	Large	Highest	Low	50 years	Low	Low	Yes
Blue-crowned conure	Loud	Medium	Some talking ability	Medium	40 years	Medium— playful	Good	No
Blue and gold macaw	Loud	Extra large	Learns words and phrases, can speak clearly	Medium	75 years	Medium— playful	Good	No
Blue-headed pionus	Low	Medium	Some ability, not clear	Low	40 years	Low	High	Yes
Bronze-winged pionus	Low	Medium	Some ability, not clear	Low	40 years	Low	High	Yes
Brown-headed parrot	Quiet	Small	Potential— squeaky voice	Low	30 years?	Medium	Good	Yes

Budgies	Quiet	Small	Males are talented—talk in high, fast voice	High	4–12 years	Low	Good	Yes
Canary	Pleasing song	Small	None	High	5–12 years	None	Highly independent	Yes
Cockatiels	Medium	Small	Males only—males whistle well	Low	15–20 years	High	Medium	Yes
Double yellow-headed Amazon	Loud	Large	Excellent	High	50+ years	Low	High	No
Dove	Soft coo	Small	None	Low	15 years	Medium	High	Yes
Eclectus	Loud	Large	Excellent talker, excellent diction	Low	50 years	Medium	High	No
Goffin's cockatoo	Loud	Medium	Good	High	40+ years	High	Medium	No
Green-cheeked conure	Quiet	Small	Some ability	Medium	30 years	Medium	High	Yes
Hahn's macaw	Medium	Medium	Can talk	Medium	40 years	Low	High	Yes

The 411 of Popular Pet Birds (cont.)

Bird Species	Loudness	Size	Talking Ability	Energy Level	Lifespan	Cuddly Quotient	Independence	Apartment Candidate
Lilac-crowned Amazon	Medium	Medium	Some talking ability	Low	40 years	Low	High	No
Lories	High	Small to large	Learn quickly and speak clearly	Very high	30–40 years	Medium	Good	No
Lovebird	Shrill	Small	None	High	10–15 years	High if hand fed	High	Yes
Maximillian pionus	Low	Medium	Some ability, not clear	Low	40 years	Low	High	Yes
Meyer's parrot	Low	Small	Squeaky voice	Medium	40 years	Low	High	Yes
Moluccan cockatoo	Extremely loud	Large	Minimal, soft voice	High	80+ years	High and needy	Low	No
Mynah	Medium	Small	Minimal, soft voice	High	10 years	Low	High	Yes
Orange-winged Amazon	Medium	Medium	Some ability	Low	40 years	Low	High	No
Parrotlets	Medium	Very small	Some	High	25–40 years	Low	High	Yes

Pionus: Maximillian, blue-headed, bronze-winged	Low	Medium	Some ability, not clear	Low	40 years	Low	High	Yes
Senegal parrot	Low	Small	Squeaky voice	Medium	40 years	Low	High	Yes
Severe macaw	High-High	Large	Good	Medium	50 years	Medium	High	No
Sun conure	Extremely loud	Medium	Some ability	Medium	30 years	Medium	High	No
Timneh African grey	Quiet	Medium	Talented talker	Low	50 years	Low	Low	Yes
Umbrella cockatoo	Loud	Large	Minimal	High	80 years	High	Low	No
Yellow-collared macaw	High-High	Large	Good	Medium	50 years	Medium	High	No
Yellow-naped Amazon	Loud	Large	Excellent	High	50+ years	Low	High	No
Zebra finches	Soft	Small	None	High	5–10 years	None	High	Yes

family is keeping his stress to a minimum. You can do this by offering your bird a diet with which he is familiar, similar waking hours (maintaining that "stable-sameness" that birds, dogs and cats seek) and by saying comforting and familiar words to him. You'll develop your own routine for care and for playing, over time. If you adopt a bird who had a previous owner, using his familiar cage and cage cover for the first month or so will help him make the adjustment.

- **Taking precautions.** If you already have avian members in your household, the first *month to six weeks* for a new bird should be a quarantine period. As prey animals, birds do not show outward signs of illness. Doing so would make them vulnerable to attack in the wild. You certainly don't want to pass on any illness your new bird may have to the existing birds in your household. During quarantine, take your new bird to an avian veterinarian for a "well-bird check" (see Chapter 2 for more details). Talk to your veterinarian about what tests are appropriate for the species and age of bird you have acquired. Quarantine should take place in a room that is *separate* from your other pet birds. For many people, this is a spare room or a bathroom. During quarantine, you should care for your new bird as though it has an infectious disease. Care for it last and do not wear the same footwear around both sets of birds. Be observant of the new bird's behavior. Definitely wash your hands after caring for the quarantined bird. Consider wearing a smock or garment to cover your clothes in the quarantine area.

- **Meeting the family.** After the quarantine is over, a new bird can then meet the other birds and get better acquainted with his new "human flock." Let birds eye each other from their *own* cages at first. **Don't ever move a new bird into the cage of an established bird!** A cage is a bird's haven and its own territory, so it is better for birds and other companion animals to meet each other in *neutral* territory, outside of their own cage. Monitor the interactions of birds with dogs and cats closely. If your predatory dog or cat is hunting your bird, you may have to keep the animals separated for safety reasons.

- **Building trust.** Spend time building trust. If your new bird is shy, then offer him treats as you go by his cage to make friends. If there are many people in your family, have *each* of them offer treats so that a relationship is established with the whole flock of people in the household.

- **Trick training to establish rapport.** (See Part 3 for more details on this.) One of the behaviors you can do with your new bird, if he will step on your hand, is to take him throughout the house. Get him used to each room and to changes in scenery. After a few hours, or days or months, depending on the tameness of the bird you have acquired, you can start working on training the "up" command, or trick training, and taking your bird into the shower with you. *All members of the family should learn how to ask your bird to step up.* If you have any indication that your bird may occasionally be aggressive, or that a member of the family is afraid of the bird, then teach your bird to step "up" onto a stick while you're working on useful commands.

Summary

Your most important goal in introducing a new pet to your home should be to make your new bird feel like a member of the family system. *Include him* in appropriate activities. *Teach him* to be quiet, to play and to accept cuddling. *Give him* what he needs, including a clean environment, healthy food, exercise and appropriate behavioral guidelines. Birds are very vocal and visual animals, so it's natural and beneficial to interact with them in vocal and visual ways. Early on, establish a "contact" call between your bird and the rest of the family (see Chapter 13) by calling out and talking to him as you travel throughout the house so he knows where you and the rest of his flock are at any given moment.

During this "getting-to-know-each-other period," take the time to read all you can about your bird's species and behavior in general. This book should go a long way in helping you do this. And you'll recognize that you and your "flock," or family system, are in for a long and wonderful adventure with your pet bird. By reading the chapters in this book and implementing what's relevant to you and your pet bird, both of you will be off to a very good start—the start of a fruitful and fulfilling relationship with your family animal. Congratulations!

CHAPTER 2

A Well-Bird Checkup

Proper Medical Care for the Life of Your Bird

The birds are moulting.
If only man could moult also—
his mind once a year its errors,
his heart once a year its useless passions.
—JAMES ALLEN (1849–1925)

File # 99-000122
Bird's Name: "Jackson"
Species: African grey parrot
Age: 10 months
Problem/Procedure: Health screening prior to purchase

"Jackson" was a young African grey parrot that was examined by a colleague of mine for a prospective buyer prior to being purchased from a reputable breeder. The physical examination and blood tests came out normal. A fecal flotation test for parasites was negative. A blood panel was sent to the laboratory to test for Psittacine Beak and Feather Disease (PBFD—a viral disease found in young parrots), Pacheco's disease (a herpes virus infection associated with hepatitis, which can be fatal in birds), and chlamydia (a bacteria-based disease associated with chronic infection). The chlamydia test came back *positive*. So, Jackson was placed into quarantine in a room with a separate ventilation system to prevent any airborne spread of the disease. The prospective owner was also advised that chlamydia is considered a "zoonosis"—an avian disease that is potentially contagious to people. However, since Jackson was an apparently healthy bird housed in a clean, low-stress environment, and provided with good nutrition, the risk of human infection was indeed very low. Both Jackson's breeder, and his prospective owner, hoped that he would ultimately pull through and completely recover from his condition.

An Ounce of Prevention Is Worth a Pound of Bird Seed

Prevention is *always* the best medicine—for **both** people and birds. The American Medical Association states that annual checkups are crucial for children ages eleven to twenty-one. *Seattle Times* reporter Laura Flynn McCarthy writes that taking your youngster for an annual "well-child" checkup allows both you and your physician to assess your child's physical and emotional development; additionally it helps the doctor get to know you and your child well enough to give the best possible care. In the mid 1980s, many of the Fortune 500 companies recognized the benefits of keeping their employees healthy through "wellness" programs that emphasized *prevention,* as opposed to paying their medical costs once they got sick (which can include medical procedures, operations, hospitalization, rehabilitation, worker's compensa-

tion, and so on). By 1985, two-thirds of the Fortune 500 companies had in-house "wellness" programs.

The American Veterinary Medical Association estimates that in
1996, $91.2 million was spent on veterinary care for pet birds.
Sixty-four percent of bird-owning homes spent at least $50 per
visit. The most common reasons for taking a pet bird to the veterinarian include (in rank order):

- an annual physical exam
- emergency care
- medication
- grooming or boarding
- advice on vitamin supplements

Visits to the emergency avian veterinary hospital may involve
costly invasive procedures and/or unnecessary trauma to your pet
bird. They can be avoided by following a straightforward well-bird
preventative health maintenance program. This Avian Wellness
program is akin to the programs that the Fortune 500 companies
have implemented for their human employees and include the
following measures:

1. A bird should have at least **one** physical examination per year
by your veterinarian. The physical examination should include:
- Weighing
- Listening to the heart and lungs
- Palpation (feeling) of the abdomen
- Checking droppings. It is best to bring the bird in the cage
  with at least two days of droppings. Also, it is wise to be
  aware of any *variation* from your bird's normal droppings.
  Droppings consist of three components: 1. Normally white
  urate crystals; 2. Clear urine; and 3. Green tubular feces.
  Changes in color and consistency of droppings suggest illness.
  For example, larger urine spots suggest a greater urine out-
  put than normal. This can occur with such illnesses as

diabetes and kidney disease. Loose droppings suggest diarrhea and possibly parasites. Yellow urates suggest liver problems.

- A Fecal Flotation Test. This is a routine test where the bird's feces is mixed with a solution that is heavier than parasitic eggs. If the bird has a parasitic infection, this will cause the ova to float to the top of the solution, which then adhere to a cover slip that seals the test container. If this happens, or if actual parasites are seen (as with coccidia), then the test is considered positive for parasitic disease.

2. Minimize physical stress/danger to your pet bird by giving it a safe and roomy cage or aviary to fly in.

3. Reduce psychological stress to your bird by giving it places to both hide behind and perch upon, to engender a sense of security and belonging.

4. Include non-toxic plants in your bird's aviary to provide natural shade and cover. This helps create a sense of privacy.

5. Do *not* allow your bird "free flight" in your house, since that will expose it to such hazards as lit stoves and transparent-looking windows. This can lead to your bird being burned, breathing in toxic fumes, or slamming head-on into your plate glass living room window and knocking itself unconscious or worse. Dr. Frank cites a case where a finch was brought to the hospital because it decided to land in a pot of simmering black bean soup! He had to be treated for burns that covered the whole lower half of his body. Not good.

6. Know the proper nutritional requirements for your species of bird and follow them to the letter (see Chapter 4).

7. Provide vitamin supplements to insure that your bird has the required minimal levels of vitamins and minerals in his diet (e.g., Vitamin D_3).

8. Provide opportunities for social interaction appropriate for your bird's species. Add other species of compatible birds to your bird's aviary in order to provide the necessary social interaction and companionship. Be observant to insure that the birds are enjoying each other's company and getting along. If you are raising a parrot without other parrots, then spend time with your parrot so that she has the social interaction she needs to be a happy member of the flock.

9. Avoid contact with outside sources of disease. If you come home after having contact with other birds, **wash your hands thoroughly with soap and hot water** *before* interacting with your own bird, to lessen the chance of transmitting a disease.

Watch for Changes in Your Bird's Routine

Frequently when parents bring their adolescent children in for family therapy with Dr. Larry, one of the first things they tell him is that they have noticed an obvious change in their youngster's customary behavior and mood. Their son or daughter has recently become withdrawn, argumentative, and unsuccessful in academic activities at school. Often, these are early warning signs of depression, anxiety, child abuse, drug/alcohol use, and/or the beginnings of a chronic or serious medical illness. Likewise, knowing what's normal and what's not with your bird's behavior—as with a parent who notices "something out of the ordinary" with his or her teenager—can be very helpful in detecting medical and behavioral problems early on.

Most birds tend to follow a regular pattern of activity and daily behavior (as with dogs and cats, who also prefer "stable-sameness" in their day-to-day routine). As with children, watch for *any* changes from your bird's normal routine; these could indicate the presence of an organic disease in its early stages. Some warning signs could include:

- A bird that does not sing or vocalize
- A bird that does not play with its toys
- A bird that appears lethargic and bored
- A bird that has forgone bathing itself

- A bird that has retreated from social interaction with either its cage mates or its human caretaker

Remember: instinctively, birds attempt to appear as normal as possible because predators look for anything abnormal and target any bird that appears weak, ill or injured—it's an evolutionary survival skill. The better you know your bird, the sooner you will detect the changes that signal the beginning of a serious medical illness.

Be Prepared
for the Veterinarian

Bring any written notes about your bird's history with you to the veterinary hospital. Try to include information on your bird's pattern of egg-laying and feather moulting (see Chapter 5). Why include this? Well, while the physical processes of both egg-laying and feather moulting are totally normal functions for birds, they can *increase* the stress that your bird may be experiencing. The increased stress from these bodily functions could manifest itself through biting and/or feather plucking (see Chapters 7 and 10). If you can describe for your vet how often your bird moults and lays its eggs, and how your pet behaves meanwhile, then your vet will really get to know your bird and provide the kind of care it needs.

To maintain its health during these periods, your bird will require additional amounts of protein and mineral supplements. If your bird is new, ask your vet to perform a chlamydia test. Many veterinarians recommend a swab test for bacteria. This is to check whether or not the right kind of bacteria are present in your bird. Your veterinarian might also recommend a group of blood tests to search for a variety of additional abnormalities. The wisest thing to do is make a written list of the following points to discuss with your bird's veterinarian during the visit:

- Any noticeable changes in either your bird's feeding or eliminating behaviors
- Any fluctuations in your bird's activity level (e.g., less active and lethargic or more active and manic)
- Any physical changes in your bird's feathers, beak, face or feet
- Any suspicious discharges coming out of your bird
- Your list of the type of food and vitamin supplements that you give your bird and how long the bird has been on these
- Your bird's health history if it has been previously treated elsewhere or has had a previous illness or injury
- Any or all medications that your bird is taking
- Any behavior problems that your bird has been exhibiting (e.g., feather plucking, screaming or biting)

Safety Tips in Handling a Sick or Injured Bird

Handling birds that are ill can pose some risk. The smaller and sicker the bird is, the *greater* the possibility that it might die from the shock of being handled. Wild birds are especially stressed by handling. To reduce the possibility of undue stress, we suggest you:

1. Have the veterinarian first observe the bird carefully from a distance.
2. Dim the lights to calm your bird and make it easier to capture for examination.
3. Speak to your bird—some tame birds will relax when they hear the voice of their owner.
4. Wrap the bird gently in a towel—this is an excellent way to calm the bird and permit a safe examination.

What Your Veterinarian Will Be Looking for in the Exam

Your veterinarian will be checking to see that:

- Your bird's feathers are smooth and densely colored. Feather deformities may result if a bird's nutrition is inadequate.
- Your bird's eyes are round and clear. Bird pupils react to light much more rapidly than mammalian (people) pupils. Often the pupils are dilated due to anxiety. Swellings above or below the eye suggest sinus problems. Sores around the beak and eyelids can be caused by the Avian Pox Virus.
- Your bird's beak is smooth and not friable. The nostrils should be inspected closely for traces of any discharge that could suggest a respiratory disease. In parakeets, the beak or face area can be scarred by an infection caused by a mange mite. This condition is called Cnemidocoptic Mange and is a parasitic infection caused by mites in parakeets. It is best treated with the drug Ivermectin.
- Your bird's toes are present in the proper number with smooth nails and a strong grip. There should be no excessive scaling, scabs or drainage on the feet.

Remember, birds do everything they can to hide their illness. So when you see a bird acting sick, he is probably much sicker than he appears to be. You need to bring him in as early as possible in the course of the illness in order to have the best chance for a successful treatment outcome.

Case Study Postscript
JACKSON

Jackson's owner chose to keep him, and his chlamydia was treated for forty-five days with the drug Doxycycline. Two weeks after the end of his treatment, another set of tests for chlamydia was carried out. This time the results were negative. The chemotherapy and quarantine treatment had worked. Jackson was well on his way to a clean bill (or beak) of health. Case closed.

CHAPTER 3

Avian "E.R."

Common Avian Illnesses and Their Treatments

*We never miss the music until the
sweet voiced bird has flown.*
—O. HENRY

File # 00-000033
Bird's Name: "Butch"
Species: Sun conure
Age: 6 months
Problem/Procedure: Victim of a dog attack

Dr. Frank reviewed a case involving a six-month-old male sun conure, whom we'll call "Butch," that had been rescued from the jaws of an attacking dog at a neighborhood pet store. Upon emergency veterinary examination, Butch seemed weak and unresponsive, but his respiration and heart rate were normal. There were no obvious signs of lacerations, punctures or broken feathers. However, while being examined, the E.R. vet discovered two gas bubbles under Butch's skin (known as subcutaneous emphysema). The vet also heard sounds of excess air coming from Butch's abdominal/chest cavity area. Butch was placed in an incubator on a low perch. A horizontal beam X ray was ordered. The X ray showed a ruptured air sac with accompanying internal bleeding. Butch had air leaking into his abdominal cavity and under his skin. Although Butch did not have any punctures or lacerations on the external layer of his skin, he still wound up with a serious internal injury from being aggressively grabbed by the attacking dog's powerful jaws.

E.R. for Birds?

In 1996, Americans made 90 million trips to emergency rooms in hospitals throughout the country. The most common reasons for going to the E.R. were loss of consciousness, signs of a heart attack or stroke, shortness of breath, bleeding, poisoning, an allergic reaction to an insect or animal bite, a major injury to the head, and persistent vomiting or vomiting up blood. Witnessing any of these symptoms in your pet bird will necessitate an **immediate** trip to the avian E.R. as well.

As mentioned in Chapter 2, the American Veterinary Medical Association estimates that close to $100 million a year is spent on veterinary treatment for pet birds. And the number-two reason why people bring their birds into the E.R. is treatment for critical injuries.

According to Dr. Margaret A. Wissman, a well-known avian veterinarian who writes for *Bird Talk* magazine, some of the top killers of pet birds include:

1. Water. Your pet bird can die of water deprivation due to a malfunctioning water bottle.

2. Unclipped wings. If you don't have your pet bird's wings clipped, it can end up flying erratically into ceiling fans or clear glass windows. Clipping the outer feathers of your bird's wings will prevent it from flying long distances at great heights.

3. Toxic fumes. The PTFE (polytetrafluoroethylene) in your Teflon or non-stick cookware can be released as a gas while cooking, causing the death of your pet bird. Common household aerosol products, such as perfume, deodorant and hairspray, can also cause respiratory problems.

4. Secondhand smoke. By inhaling cigarette, cigar or pipe smoke, your pet bird (as with your pet dog or cat) can develop eye problems, skin irritation and respiratory disease.

5. Trauma. If your bird climbs down from its cage and starts walking around the floor, he is putting himself in grave danger of being stepped on, sat on, crushed in a closing door or in bed if sleeping with its owner, or though it may sound impossible, being vacuumed up during household chores.

6. Other animals. As with the story of Butch in the beginning of this chapter, birds can sustain fatal injuries by being chased, pounced upon, shaken or bitten by either a household companion animal or a stray dog or cat. For example, dogs, cats and other animals can kill your bird either through the bacteria (Pasteurella) that live in their saliva, or by clawing your bird and causing severe injuries that result in toxic shock. Avian E.R. vets recommend that if your bird has been attacked or teased by an animal, always assume that your pet has been bitten and seek veterinary assistance *immediately!*

7. Toxic food or plants. There are several foods that are dangerous for your bird. Chocolate, caffeine, some varieties of avocado and possibly onions can be very toxic, potentially fatal for your feathered family animal. There are also many poisonous plants you should keep out of your house, or at least away from your bird's cage, including dieffenbachia, lily of the valley, philodendron, poinsettia, rhododendron, foxglove (the source for digitalis), amaryllis, azalea, clematis, daffodil, ivy, holly, hydrangea, iris, larkspur, lobelia, marijuana, mistletoe, monkshood, morning glory, narcissus, nightshades, privet, sweet pea, lupines, oleander and tobacco.

8. Heat exposure. Your bird can die from hyperthermia—heat stroke or heat exhaustion—either by being left in the car or put outside in its cage in a shady spot in the morning, only to literally "shake and bake" by the afternoon when the shade has dissipated and the full unforgiving glare of the sun is bearing down. As Dr. Wissman writes, most birds suffering from hyperthermia will try to get out of the sun, and may try to bathe to cool off, if possi-

---

Pet Bird Safety Checklist

- Do you know where your cat or dog is at all times?
- Are all your doors and windows screened or closed?
- Are the toilet lids down and aquariums covered?
- Are the stove jets turned off when not in use?
- Are containers of cleaners, paint or other toxic substances sealed and put away?
- Are all ceiling fans turned off before your bird leaves its cage?
- Are electrical cords, phone lines or wiring out of your bird's reach?
- Have you closed or put away cosmetics and perfumes?
- Will you be able to keep an eye on your bird every second it's out of its cage?
- Have you made sure *everyone* knows the bird is out, so no one will step or sit on it?
- Are unsafe plants out of reach?
- Are all toxic foods (like avocado or chocolate) put away?
- Have you emptied or removed all containers with liquid in them? This will prevent your bird from flying into a container of liquid and drowning.

ble. However, if the bird cannot escape the heat of the sun, it will have a seizure and die.

Avian Red Cross: Urgent Signs That Your Bird Needs First Aid!

If you ever spot your bird at the bottom of its cage acting ill or injured you can be certain your bird needs medical care right away. Bring your bird to an avian E.R. as soon as possible. Watch closely to see if your bird's tail is bobbing up and down with each breath it takes. A bobbing tail indicates a respiratory problem and should be treated promptly. Other signs that your pet bird needs immediate medical attention include any unusual discharges coming from its eyes or nose in addition to sneezing or coughing. If the weather is warm but your bird has its feathers all fluffed up, this is also an indicator that your bird is ill or injured and requires immediate veterinary care.

If your pet bird does end up being injured, traumatized or acutely ill—requiring first-aid or emergency treatment—what can you do? Dr. Frank provides the following suggestions:

- Remain calm.
- Ask for assistance from friends and family members if possible.
- See if you can determine the problem:

1. Breathing difficulties. If your bird is not breathing, use artificial respiration by blowing into its nostrils while holding the mouth shut. This is a heroic measure, and sometimes it works. (Certainly any bird that needs artificial respiration needs veterinary care as soon as possible. After this, your bird would need oxygen, and injections to stimulate its heart for treatment of shock.)
2. Bleeding. If your bird is bleeding, apply gentle direct pressure. Be sure the bird can breathe by expanding his chest from front to back. Hold the bird from the side so the chest can go out

and back. If you cover your bird's eyes, it may help him to relax during this ordeal.

3. Bloody feathers. If your bird has bloodied feathers, this may indicate that they are damaged. A damaged and bleeding feather must be removed or it will continue to bleed. Remove it gently and carefully with tweezers. Have some styptic powder on hand to stop the bleeding and apply it with a Q-tip. In addition to styptic powder, your avian first-aid kit should contain a towel to cover, calm, and restrain your bird if necessary. Monitor your bird for an hour after the bleeding has stopped to make sure it doesn't start up again. If the bleeding resumes or does not stop, have someone else drive you to the veterinarian so you can continue to apply gentle pressure to the bleeding area while seeking help. For finches and canaries, you can cup them in your hands, which provide needed warmth and block out excessive stress-inducing light. You can also wrap them in a towel, or place them in a warm towel-lined box to take them to the avian E.R.

4. Fractures and broken bones. If you have a small parakeet, use micropore tape to immobilize fractures or broken bones. It is an excellent tape because it does not stick to your bird's feathers and it's light and strong. For larger birds with bigger fractures, Dr. Frank recommends that you use a roll of Vetwrap. Vetwrap is a lightweight elastic bandage that sticks only to itself and is ideal for immobilizing an injured wing. A wing can be folded and bandaged around your bird's body. Wrap the injured wing in a figure-eight pattern, then loosely apply the wrap around the body to allow your bird's chest to rise and fall for adequate breathing. Also, while holding your bird, be careful not to crush it or prevent its chest from moving. Dr. Frank has seen birds asphyxiate because a well-meaning rescuer or owner held them so tightly they could not breathe. A bird's broken bones heal quickly. A parakeet's broken leg will fully heal in approximately 10 days if it is immobilized properly with wrapping.

5. Convulsions. A convulsion is a series of erratic motor movements and sensations caused by abnormal electrical dis-

Your Avian First-Aid Kit

In addition to Vetwrap and micropore tape, any good avian first-aid kit, or supply bin, should include the following items:

- **Hydrogen peroxide**—which helps to clean wounds.
- **A clamping device**—similar to a surgical clamp called a hemostat, to control bleeding.
- **Various size syringes**—to be used for hand feeding your bird.
- **A safe bird carrier**—Use a covered bird carrier to provide sufficient warmth in transporting your sick or injured bird to the veterinary hospital or avian E.R. Any suitably sized enclosure will do (like a shoebox or a cage with the perches removed). For a cold bird in shock you can construct a "bird waterbed" to help keep it warm, by using a Ziploc bag filled with warm water for it to lie on, heated to around 87 degrees (creating an accompanying humidity level of 75 percent). This is considered the ideal temperature for most ill birds.
- **Surgical gauze pads**—to apply pressure on a wound to control bleeding. In a pinch, any cloth or T-shirt will work.

charges in the brain, manifested by twitching and muscle spasms throughout the body. During convulsions or seizures, your bird may fall off its perch and it may appear disoriented when the episode is over. Convulsions last from a few seconds to several minutes. If your pet bird is having convulsions, place it in an environment where it cannot injure itself. If kept in a cage, remove perches, toys and dishes (as you would do with furniture and sharp objects for a family member or friend who is having a seizure). Pad the cage with a towel. Dim the lights or cover the cage after the seizure has passed. Maintain a quiet warm environment. Take your bird to your veterinarian or local avian E.R. as soon as you can.

6. Cat bites. Cat bites are always an emergency for your pet bird. Shock can occur even if there are no obvious wounds. Such wounds can be difficult to see. Any time your bird has been in a cat's mouth, assume it has been bitten. Look for external bleeding and apply pressure if needed. Usually most of the injuries are inside and antibiotic therapy may be needed to save your bird's life. As discussed earlier, cats carry many types of bacteria in their saliva and their bites frequently become infected. If your pet bird is bitten by a cat or dog, place it in a warm enclosed container with something soft like a towel inside, and take it immediately to the avian E.R. Do everything you can to minimize the stress for your favorite feathered friend. One of Dr. Frank's clients would sing to her parrot when the bird was frightened and it would relax almost immediately.

7. Egg binding. Egg binding occurs when the bird, or hen, is unable to lay an egg. The egg is literally "bound" and stuck. Outward signs of avian egg binding include lethargy or depression, and straining. Less frequent signs are abdominal distention (bloating), leg weakness, difficulty in breathing and sometimes sudden death. A vet will make an egg-binding diagnosis based on the symptoms listed above, in addition to feeling for the egg in the abdomen or taking an ultrasound exam or X-ray. If you think your bird is suffering from egg-binding, apply moderately warm steam to the bird by holding her about a foot or so over a lightly boiling tea kettle for *only 3 to 5 minutes.* **Caution: Do not hold the bird longer than this or closer to the kettle! You can badly burn and injure your bird! If you are not comfortable holding your bird, do not attempt to apply steam!** The goal is to raise the immediate environmental temperature around your egg-bound bird to around 85 to 90 degrees. If your bird produces an egg within thirty to sixty minutes, then there is no need to worry. Otherwise take her to the avian E.R. for prompt intervention.

8. Heat stroke. One of the top killers of pet birds is heat stroke or heat exhaustion. As mentioned above, this frequently happens when a bird is left in the car unattended or its cage (with the bird inside) is placed outside in a shady spot that, over a period of time, loses its shade and becomes as hot as a blowtorch. If you suspect that your bird is overheated or is suffering from hyperthermia, remove the bird *immediately* to a cool area. If it is still conscious, spray its feathers with water, immerse its feet in cold water, and allow the bird to drink sufficient amounts of water. All these measures will help lower your bird's excessive body temperature. After these immediate steps, place your bird in a soft towel-lined box to ensure its comfort and safety and take it immediately to the avian E.R.

9. Poisoning. If your bird has ingested poison, you will need to contact the ASPCA's National Animal Poison Control Center right away (1-800-548-2423 or 1-888-4ANIHELP/1-888-426-4435). Again, immediate veterinary medical assistance is essential in this situation. The best way to deal with poisons is to prevent access to them whenever possible. Purchase stainless steel or brass cages and avoid painted cages and bowls and poisonous houseplants.

By following the safety checklist and eliminating the potential hazards that are the top killers of birds, it is our hope that you and your pet bird will *never* experience such a severe or life-threatening injury. However if you do, then we hope Dr. Frank's first-aid tips will help save your bird's life if and when the situation or crisis arises.

If Your Bird Doesn't Survive Its Injury—Pet Loss and the Grieving Process

Pet loss is a legitimate loss often involving various reactions, stages or phases of grief. These phases may include rage, guilt, terror, fear, denial, sadness, anger, anxiety, loneliness, fatigue, shock, numbness or relief.

To move through the most painful and debilitating parts of your grief, Dr. Larry suggests the following steps:

- *Feel your feelings.* Feel what you are feeling instead of stuffing feelings with alcohol, drugs or throwing yourself incessantly into your work.
- *Create a protective emotional cocoon.* Surround yourself with supportive people who won't make light of your loss.
- *Relieve the pressure of the volcano of grief.* Talk about it. Cry.
- *Honor the importance of your loss.* Ritualize the loss by creating a "rite of passage," by holding a graveside memorial service, putting together a photo album, organizing a family get-together, or taping a farewell song or video.
- *Be patient with your process.* Allow time to heal. We tend *to grieve as deeply as we loved.* And our love for our pet bird did not appear overnight. It was built over time, and so it will take time for the hurt and pain to subside.
- *Extra nurturing for extra stress.* Get sufficient rest and nutrition. Remember that grieving is fatiguing. Your mind and body are under incredible stress—not unlike a soldier in combat or an Olympic athlete recovering from a grueling competition. During grief, it is not unusual for your body's adrenal glands to release fight/flight stress hormones that cause your brain's mood chemicals (serotonin, norepinephrine and acetylcholine) to be reduced, leading to down-in-the-dumps feelings along with an increase in production of your body's own pain-relieving substances, called *endorphins.* The elevated endorphin release can stimulate appetite, coinciding with what Dr. Larry's current bereavement group members tell him—that during their mourning period, they begin to overeat or eat sugary foods in order to feel better.
- *Put things in perspective and take your grief seriously.* Take off from work whatever time is needed.

- *Reach out to others in the same boat.* Consider joining a bereavement or pet-loss group in your area.

Finally, here's a poem that Peggy Kurth wrote in memory of her parakeet, Henry:

HENRY

Henry was my parakeet.
She is always with me, but I never see her.
Her squawks and chirps were very sweet.
She is always with me, but I never see her.
Henry hated to be left alone in her cage.
She is always with me, but I never see her.
When I read a book, she would chew every page.
She is always with me, but I never see her.
I had her for almost a year.
She is always with me, but I never see her.
Henry didn't have even one fear.
She is always with me, but I never see her.
Her feathers were yellow and blue.
She is always with me, but I never see her.
Both colors were a very beautiful hue.
She is always with me, but I never see her.
And then last October, she was gone.
She is always with me, but I never see her.
In my hands, she passed on.
She is always with me, but I never see her.
—PEGGY KURTH

Case Study Postscript
BUTCH

To treat Butch's injuries, the E.R. vet prescribed antibiotics to fight off any possible infection stemming from the bacteria in the dog's saliva. Butch was also fed through a stomach tube (called a "gavage") every twelve hours for seven days. By the third day, Butch was starting to eat, and by the fourteenth day, the air under his skin had all been reabsorbed and the damaged air sacs healed. With excellent avian E.R., Butch thankfully made a full recovery. Case closed.

CHAPTER 4

Canary Cuisine

Your Bird's Nutritional and Dietary Needs

Does the Eagle know what is in the pit?
Or wilt thou go ask the Mole?
Can Wisdom be put in a silver rod,
Or Love in a golden bowl?
—WILLIAM BLAKE (1757–1827), *The Book of Thel*

CASE 1
File # 89-000557
Bird's Name: "Terry"
Species: Umbrella cockatoo
Age: 2 years
Problem/Procedure: Malnutrition*

---

* Thanks to Brian Speer, D.V.M., of the Veterinary Information Network, for this case example.

"Terry" was a young umbrella cockatoo, brought into the emergency veterinary clinic, who was having difficulty breathing (dyspnea) and exhibiting general weakness. In taking a history, the veterinarian learned that Terry's diet mainly consisted of potato chips, mashed potatoes, pretzels, baby food, cod liver oil, and a calcium supplement. Knowing that Terry was seriously ill and that they were running out of time, the avian E.R. staff began prepping him for an infusion of nutrients and antibiotics. They hoped that it was not too late to help Terry and his owner.

CASE 2
File # 96-001019
Bird's Name: "Ned"
Species: Lilac-crowned Amazon
Age: 20 years
Problem/Procedure: Malnutrition-induced high cholesterol

"Ned," a twenty-year-old male lilac-crowned Amazon, was also brought into the veterinary emergency clinic for treatment of pronounced lethargy. Upon taking a medical history, the vet learned that Ned had been fed an exclusively seed-based diet. Blood tests showed that Ned had significantly elevated cholesterol levels. The veterinary staff suspected that Ned's elevated cholesterol was a result of his diet and they were determined to lower his cholesterol to a more acceptable and safe level.

We Are What We Eat! Nutrition and Health in People and Birds

The National Center for Health Statistic's 1999 health and nutrition survey showed that an estimated 61 percent of adults in the United States are either overweight or obese. Poor diet contributes to five of the ten leading causes of death in the United States.

Nutrition experts Covert Bailey, in his book *The New Fit or Fat*, and Cliff Sheats, in his book *Lean Bodies,* stress the point that even though a person may weigh about the same at forty as he did at twenty, he may nevertheless be more fat. Sheats says that all of his clients have two things in common: they are not eating enough food to fuel their bodies, and, what little food they do eat is the wrong kind of food. These two factors are also responsible for cases of malnutrition in pet birds. Birds that are not eating enough food, or are not getting the *right kind of food,* frequently face the same ailments that people do that all too often lead to a premature death.

Polly Want a Cracker?
How About Pellets and
Veggies Instead?

Ninety percent of physical ailments in pet birds are caused by malnutrition. In birds, nutritional requirements vary with each species as well as with the particular bird's age, activity level, reproductive activity, stress level and surrounding climate.

For example, nectar-loving birds such as lorikeets do better with high levels of nectar (high in sugar) in their diets. African grey parrots are famous for needing more dietary calcium than most other parrots. A small parrot needs to have 15 to 20 percent of its diet made up of protein while growing, and only 10 to 14 percent later as an adult. Pigeons need more calories when they are racing. Egg-laying birds need more calcium and molting birds need more protein. In warm weather, birds need more water and in cold weather they need more calories. By educating yourself about the basic nutritional requirements of your pet bird, you can successfully avoid the health risks described at the beginning of the chapter in the unfortunate cases of Terry and Ned.

Avoiding Bird Malnutrition: Things Every Bird Owner Should Know

As we discussed above, nutritional imbalances occur if your bird receives *too much* or *too little* of the nutrition he needs. Most of our pet birds are only a few generations removed from the wild. A good diet nourishes healthy birds with vibrant feathers, strong vigorous bodies and healthy offspring. Proper nutritional care for your family's fine feathered friend should include the following:

- **Water.** Water is crucial to health. It should be free of contaminants and impurities. Avoid placing the perches over the water bowl (or you can literally end up with "poopy" water) and change the water frequently. Be sure there is always lots of water available, and use fresh bottled if you can. Salt contained in water softening systems has been attributed to causing a high mortality in baby birds two to ten days of age.
- **Pelleted foods.** Pelleted foods have the advantage over seed-only diets because they contain all the known required nutrients for a particular species of bird. Pelleted foods tend to be well fortified with vitamins and minerals, which means your bird will be less likely to suffer from malnutrition on a pellet food diet.
- **Fresh food supplements.** It is wise to supplement a pelleted diet with a variety of fresh foods. For example, psitticines benefit from supplementing their formulated diet with vegetables, fruit, and whole grains. When you're not choosing produce, try to purchase freshly made foods. They tend to be richer in nutrients than older or stale foods. Look for a date of manufacture, sometimes referred to as the "mill date." Foods manufactured within ninety days of purchase are preferred. Make sure you buy your bird's food from a store with a high turnover of food stock.

Turning Your Bird into the Energizer Bunny: Bird Food for Energy

There are *three* main sources of energy that your bird needs in order to remain healthy. They are *fats, carbohydrates* and *proteins.* Fat provides twice the calories per unit of weight of either carbohydrate or protein. Birds prefer high energy foods like seeds, which are rich in fats (as we do with hamburgers, fries and ice cream). Therefore a high fat diet needs a higher concentration of other essential nutrients like vitamins to offset what your pet bird may be missing out on. Fat is essential in *small* quantities; a fat deficiency in birds is rare, but excess is common. Obesity is a surprisingly *common* occurrence in pet birds, especially with parakeets. Obesity places extra strain on your bird's heart, it increases anesthesia risk by limiting chest expansion during respiration, and it is also associated with infertility. Obesity in birds has been known to cause confusing X-ray findings as well, producing false-positive readings for an enlarged liver. The good thing about fat is that it is an excellent source of vitamin E, which your bird's body needs. In chickens, vitamin E deficiency leads to brain softening (encephalomalacia) and muscle disease. This deficiency will develop in pet birds, too, if their diets are poor. You should consider levels of vitamin E and selenium together when evaluating your bird's diet.

It's helpful to find out your bird's ideal weight from your veterinarian and weigh the bird from time to time on a kitchen scale. With your hand, feel the area over your bird's breastbone and abdomen for excessive fat deposits. Sometimes you can even hear a parakeet wheezing when it is excited, due to the high levels of body fat buildup.

If you want to help your bird lose body fat, here are some good suggestions:

1. Provide more exercise opportunities, beginning with a larger flight cage.
2. Increase social interaction with your bird and give him toys to engage him in play more often.
3. Feed your bird a lower-calorie diet, one that has less fat and more vegetables.
4. Limit your bird's feedings, *but be careful because birds need to eat frequently.*

"One-A-Day" for Parrots? Vitamin Supplements for Your Pet Bird

Green foods tend to be rich in vitamin A; this is why a seed-only diet could cause a deficiency. Vitamin A deficiency can result in impaired vision and infection. Be sure your bird gets both a vitamin-supplemented pelleted ration and some leafy green vegetables. One way to give the vegetables is to place them on the top wire of the cage so the bird can peck at them and pull them into the cage. Many birds find this fun.

Most pet birds need a special kind of vitamin D called vitamin D_3 (cholecalciferol). Mammals can make D_3 with sunlight, *but birds cannot!* Vitamin D enhances calcium metabolism in the body, so a deficiency of this vitamin often causes rickets, a condition that presents as weak and crooked bones. On the other hand, too much vitamin D (toxicity) can lead to kidney failure. Talk with your vet about the correct dosage of vitamin D_3, or the correct portion of vitamin D_3-enriched foods, for your bird.

Vitamin K is necessary for normal blood clotting. Some species of birds, like fig parrots, need much more vitamin K than other birds. If their diet lacks high levels of vitamin K, they can hemorrhage and die because their blood won't clot properly.

Niacin is an essential component of your bird's nutrition. The amino acid tryptophan is the building block for niacin, but very little is found in corn, so birds on 100 percent corn diets are at risk for niacin deficiency. In chickens, this deficiency is called pellagra or "black tongue" disease. It is better that corn be only *a part* of your pet bird's diet. Extra niacin may be needed to compensate for any corn-induced deficiencies in your pet's nutritional profile.

In chickens, riboflavin deficiency produces deformed or curly toes. In cockatiels, it is associated with loss of color pigment of the wing feathers. Extra riboflavin is also needed for healthy egg production. Breeding cockatiels produce and hatch fewer eggs when their diets are not supplemented with riboflavin.

Bird diets deficient in vitamin B_{12} can cause anemia, gizzard erosion, fatty heart, fatty liver and fatty kidneys. Plants contain no B_{12} so most bird diets require supplementation with B_{12} to maintain good health and a long life.

Cockatiels, hummingbirds, ducks and chickens can make their own vitamin C. Unless you are sure your bird can make his own vitamin C, supplementation is prudent.

Calcium levels in pet birds is a controversial subject, but most doctors agree that all birds need some amount of calcium for strong bones, strong egg shells, and other functions. For most pet birds, the general recommended figure for calcium in the diet is .5 percent, and remember, maintaining healthy levels of vitamin D_3 will increase your bird's calcium absorption. The amount of phosphorus in the diet also affects calcium metabolism. In this case, however, phosphorus blocks absorption of calcium instead of boosting it. Except during egg production, the ratio of calcium to phosphorus in your bird's diet should be 2 to 1.

Traditionally, seed-only diets had caused severe goiters, or growths, in parakeets before doctors began to use iodine supplements. Iodine is an essential part of the thyroxin (thyroid hormone) molecule. Without enough iodine, the thyroid gland enlarges and eventually develops into a goiter.

If your bird's diet lacks sufficient salt or sodium, this could stunt its growth, limit egg production during egg-laying, and even cause cannibalism. A salt block with trace minerals is one way to prevent this problem. Or, you can make sure your bird's pellet food contains adequate sodium. Talk to your vet about the best option.

Nutritional Hazards for Your Bird

It is important to know not only what nutrients your bird *needs* to remain healthy, but also what hidden nutritional dangers to *avoid*. Here are those you should be particularly aware of:

- **Lactose (milk sugar).** Birds cannot digest lactose, so no dairy products for birds.
- **Preservative spoilage.** Spoiled bird food will have a reduced nutrient content and could introduce harmful organisms to your bird's body.
- **Excess moisture.** Moisture in stored foods encourages fungal growth that can also be harmful to your pet. Keep your bird's food as dry as possible and buy your bird's pellet food before the sell-by date.

"Give It to Mikey—He'll Eat It!": Coping with a Finicky Eater

Often, caged and aviary birds display strong preferences for particular foods like sunflower seeds (avian junk food!) that are not all that good for them. If these foods make up a large part of their diet, they can become malnourished. If your pet bird has been on a junk diet (as in Terry's case at the beginning of the chapter), or a deficient seed-only diet for most of its life (as with Ned), then how can you convince your bird to eat a more nutritious pelleted diet?

First, your bird needs to recognize that the pellets are indeed food. The good news is birds like cockatiels will accept new kinds of foods usually within a 48-hour period. Many veterinary journals recount cases in which 90 percent of birds who initially refused the new, more nutritious food, and were put back on the familiar junk diet accepted the healthy food when it was reintroduced two weeks later. Persistence can pay off!

Here are some tips on how to get your "fast-food" feathered friend to eat better:

- **Phase in/phase out.** Gradually add more of the nutritious pellets to the junk food ration. The bird food manufacturer Kaytee recommends the following phase-in ratios:

  Days 1 to 3—75 percent old and 25 percent new food
  Days 4 to 6—50 percent old and 50 percent new food
  Days 7 to 10—25 percent old and 75 percent new food

- **Induce jealousy and mimicry.** Just like the commercial that depicted the other kids wanting the cereal after "Mikey" ate it, another useful technique to get your bird to eat better is to have it observe other birds consuming the new pellets so they learn to recognize them as food. Your bird will begin to eat the pellets so as to not be left out of the flock activity.

- **Use recommended brands.** Stick to well-established and widely recognized high-quality bird food manufacturers to maximize your chances that your pet bird will easily "convert" to a more nutritious diet. Some of the best manufacturers of good quality nutritious foods include Roudybush, Harrison's Bird diets, Kaytee and Lafeber.

For more information on avian nutrition and quality food manufacturers, visit *http://www.kaytee.com*, *http://www.roudybush. com* and *http://www.waltham.com*

Case Studies Postscript
TERRY

Despite treatment with antibiotics, fluids, corticosteroids, and placement in an incubator, Terry the cockatoo died shortly after being admitted to the avian E.R. An autopsy found that Terry had dead tissue in his liver, spleen and heart, in addition to built-up congestion in his lungs and swelling of fatty tissues throughout his body. There was no evidence of infectious disease. The tentative diagnosis was severe and fatal vitamin E deficiency. Could proper nutrition have prevented Terry's untimely passing? Probably so.

NED

It was believed that Ned's high cholesterol levels were caused by his solely seed-based diet. Many seed-based diets can also lead to mineral imbalances, obesity, a fatty liver, vitamin A or essential amino acid deficiencies. To combat his high cholesterol levels, Ned's diet had to completely change. A phase-out of seeds and a phase-in of nutritionally formulated pellets and fresh vegetables was what the doctor ordered. Unlike Terry, Ned was thankfully saved in the nick of time. Case closed.

CHAPTER 5

Sex and the Single Parakeet

Sexuality and Breeding Basics

Let the great bird of love loft in your being.
Let it alight in the unknowing crevices of the spirit . . .
—D. N. SUTTON, "Great Bird"

CASE 1
File # 01-001013
Bird's Name: "Lizzy"
Species: African grey parrot
Age: 18 months
Problem/Procedure: Mate-induced vomiting*

* Thanks to Carol Helfer, D.V.M, and Ilana Reisner, D.V.M., of the Veterinary
Information Network, for this case example.

"Lizzy" was an eighteen-month-old African grey parrot that began throwing up her food whenever she was around her owner. Generally a friendly and tame bird, Lizzy shared a close bond with her owner. Other than her throwing up, Lizzy appeared healthy and well adjusted. Lizzy's owner, frightened and concerned, decided to consult a veterinarian about her condition. She fervently hoped that the vet could help make Lizzy better.

CASE 2
File # 01-001021
Bird's Name: "Amy"
Species: Cinnamon-pied cockatiel
Age: 3 years
Problem/Procedure: Distended oviduct causing open mouth breathing

"Amy" was a three-year-old female hand-raised cinnamon-pied cockatiel, who had been taken to the hospital because of excessive open mouth breathing and loss of appetite. Her owner had been treating Amy's food for a week with a spray for respiratory infections. However, her condition remained unchanged. In addition, Amy had not laid an egg for five months. Getting more and more concerned, Amy's owner brought her to the veterinarian for a complete physical. She was determined to get to the bottom of what was going on with her beloved Amy.

Sex and Courting in People and Birds: Dr. Ruth, Where Are You?

According to Carol Stacy, publisher of *Romantic Times Magazine,* 1,800 new romance titles are published each year: that is, 53 percent of all mass-market fiction purchased in the United States, generating $1 billion in annual sales. Clearly, birds aren't the only ones preoccupied with romance and sex.

The renowned sex therapists Dr. William Masters and Dr. Virginia Johnson are credited for outlining what is known as the

"Human Sexual Response Cycle." In order for a person to have sex, he or she must successfully go through *four* phases of emotional and physical response. They are:

1. *The desire phase.* The urge to be romantic or have sex.
2. *The excitement phase.* The physiological changes in our bodies, including increased heart rate, blood pressure and muscle tension, to physically mate.
3. *The orgasm phase.* Where an individual's sexual pleasure peaks and tension is released through involuntary rhythmic muscle contractions.
4. *The resolution phase.* Where the parties involved return to a resting state equal to how they were prior to entering the desire phase. The body and mind relax and wind down.

What people and birds have in common is that we both use the singular "courting techniques" in creating the right mood for romance and sex. Both people and birds tend to do the following things prior to mating:

- We take our romantic partners out to eat or drink.
- We take our romantic partners out dancing.
- We engage in silly "play."
- We buy flashy new clothes and show off our "feathers."
- We take our romantic partners to a private cozy area or nest.
- We engage in a lot of non-sexual, and then sexual, touching (which psychologists and ornithologists alike refer to as "tactile stimulation").
- We watch intently for non-verbal cues (an eyebrow here, a raised wing there).
- We are obsessed with "doing it" in the right position or on the right perch.
- We kiss (mouth to mouth or rub beak to beak).
- And we "scare away" the competition with threatening behavior.

One of the courting behaviors Dr. Larry listed above was the ability of the couple in question to "play" with each other. To set the appropriate mood, and to establish a give-and-take relationship in advance of intimacy, we must be able to play with our partners. When Dr. Larry sees couples for marriage counseling, it is almost without exception that the people before him have stopped "playing." Part of what Dr. Larry does is bring the couple back to that time of courting, and have them rediscover some of the recreational and "fun" things that initially brought them together. It seems that people, as well as birds (as we'll see below), require specific courting and mating rituals to both get in the mood for sex and to be able to mate successfully.

Parakeet Courtship: Check Out My New Duds, Sweetie!

During courting and mating, the male parakeet sings to his female companion while puffing up his feathers on his head and throat. Often parakeets preen each other's feathers and kiss by rubbing their beaks together. Bonded pairs of parakeets are often seen sitting together rubbing beaks. The male then feeds his mate by regurgitating up some food from his crop (thanks for sharing). This ritual feeding seems to calm aggressive or frightened female partners. Then, *if* the female accepts him (it had better be a good dinner), she permits him to mate with her. She will then fluff her feathers and raise her tail in return. The male first moves alongside of the female, and then he lifts one leg and stands momentarily on her back with one of his feet. Then he mounts the female and lowers his tail while covering her with his own wings. (Where's that "do not disturb" sign?)

Cockatiel Courtship: The Tony Bennett Way!

During courting and mating, the male cockatiel *sings* a two-note melody for *long* periods of time to woo his female partner. During mating, it is recommended that cockatiel owners provide a cardboard nesting box ranging in size from 12 × 12 × 12 inches to 12 × 12 × 16 inches, with a 4-inch square opening. Sometimes the male "leads" the female to the nest box while singing (happy fellow). While the male sings, he bobs his head and makes a silent chattering movement with his beak. The female responds with silent chattering and mating ensues either in the nest box or on the perch.

Canary Courtship: Don Juan or Jenny Craig? Make Up Your Mind

Canary courtship begins with good food. A canary owner also needs to provide good nutrition, room to exercise and a comfortable enclosure for their breeding pet. A nesting box about 3.5 inches square and 2 inches deep sets the mood.

Typically, the male canary is placed in a cage next to the female, divided only by a partition with multiple holes that allow the birds to see each other. Usually within five to seven days, the male canary begins to feed the female through these holes in the partition. The male then pulls his feathers against his body and serenades the female vigorously ("I left my heart in . . .") When the female is ready, she begins to carry around nesting material, raises her tail when on the perch, and calls out to the male. Now is the time to remove the partition . . . and take your dog for a walk.

Timing Is Indeed Everything

Timing is everything in a successful mating. Although people seem to prefer total darkness or romantic candlelight, our pet birds prefer to see exactly what is going on. Light, it seems, is one of the most important factors in triggering reproductive activity in birds.

For example, cockatiels and blossom-headed parakeets are both stimulated to reproduce and mate by long periods of sunlight. (Alaska in the summer, here we come!) If the light is sufficient for a person to read a book, then it is strong enough to set off sexual activity in your light-sensitive bird. The thyroid gland and its hormone are believed to be the influence on this light-induced behavior.

"The Birds and the Bees": Laying and Hatching

Most adult birds have only one ovary—or at least only one that is discernable: the left one. Both male and female gonads enlarge and regress seasonally. In the female, egg yolks of various sizes cling to the ovary and make it easy to distinguish her from the male. The female bird reproductive tract consists of:

- An ovary
- The oviduct
- Isthmus and magnum structures that produce the protein albumen, making up the white part of the developing egg for protection and nutrient value for the developing chick
- A uterus (or shell gland)

Fertilization occurs in the oviduct. As a fertilized ovum travels down the oviduct, the rest of the egg forms around it. Eggs spend variable periods of time in the vagina before laying occurs. If they get stuck in the oviduct, this results in egg binding, discussed in Chapter 3.

Once the bird lays its eggs, there is a period of incubation leading up to hatching. A fertile egg consists of an outer shell surrounding an embryo and yolk, suspended in a layer of albumen protein. Outside the albumen are external and internal shell membranes. The albumen and the yolk nourish the embryo as it grows to become a chick. By the time laying occurs, the embryo will have anywhere from two hundred to six thousand cells, depending on the bird species. As the embryo grows, membranes develop around it, containing blood vessels which exchange oxygen and carbon dioxide through the porous shell.

"Let Me Out of Here!": Hatchability

Breeders measure the percentage of eggs that are fertile compared to the percentage of eggs that actually do hatch to come up with the concept of "hatchability." To determine if an egg is fertile, an aviculture breeder will pass a light through the laid egg and look for a dark area surrounded by a red vascular ring of blood vessels. If this is absent, then the egg is not fertile.

One of the possible problems that can crop up with a developing bird fetus is that bacteria can migrate through the pores in the eggshell. Therefore, incubating eggs should be kept as *clean* as possible. Breeders and veterinarians recommend using clean or gloved hands to handle eggs. Make sure you maintain a clean environment for your bird to minimize the fecal material around the eggs. Egg washing in warm water or a diluted disinfectant, such as 1 percent povidone iodine, is useful to remove any visible fecal matter than can serve as a source of contamination to the developing chick while it is still in the egg.

Egg weight tends to decline during incubation due to water and carbon dioxide loss through the eggshell. The rate of weight loss depends on temperature, humidity, and the number and size of pores in the eggshell. The typical weight loss is 13 percent of initial weight, with a range of possible total weight loss being 11 to 16 percent. A good "artificial" incubator turns the eggs at least five times daily. Bird parents, the "natural" incubators, turn the eggs about every thirty-five minutes. Turning the eggs prevents the embryo from becoming stuck to the shell, and allows the chick to position itself properly in the shell for eventual hatching.

"Move Over—Here I Come!": The Arrival

When a chick hatches from its egg, carbon dioxide levels rise and cause spasms in the chick's neck muscles, forcing its beak to puncture the air cell that lies at one end of the egg so that its head can enter it. This creates a second source of air for breathing (the other is the network of membranes connected through the egg's pores). When the carbon dioxide level approaches 10 percent concentration, the chick's muscle spasms become stronger and it will thrust its beak through the actual eggshell, now creating a hole that increases the overall air circulation for the chick. The time from perforating the air cell and pecking through the eggshell varies from three hours to three days, with most pet bird species taking twenty-four to forty-eight hours to get there.

Avian "Gender Identity Disorder": Who the Heck Am I?

Determining the sex of your pet bird can be like having Lieutenant Columbo trying to solve a murder mystery while in a coma: very difficult indeed. However, one way to determine the sex of a pet bird is to examine secondary sexual characteristics such as the blue cere nostrils on a male parakeet. Female parakeets lack this blue coloring. However, many birds are sexually "monomorphic," or indistinguishable, which can make breeding a challenge.

Another way to determine a pet bird's sex is with exploratory surgery to see if the bird in question has reproductive organs. Although this method is accurate, it is invasive and carries the risk of complications from anesthesia and infection. Veterinarians may also conduct chromosomal analysis to find out a bird's sex. This works regardless of a bird's age and does not involve anesthetic risk to the bird. It does, however, require expert laboratory analysis. This analysis has an accuracy rate of 68 to 100 percent. So, don't bet the farm (or aviary) on it. In chromosomal analysis, the investigator is looking for Z or W chromosomes. (Did you learn that in your high school biology class?) Female birds have a Z and a W chromosome, and males have two W chromosomes. This is the opposite in mammals, where the male has the *different* set of chromosomes, X and Y, and the female has two of the same.

One of the most popular and accurate ways of testing your pet bird's sex is through DNA analysis. The test is called the Restriction Fragment Length Polymorphism test (RFLP for short). This test is nearly 100 percent accurate. The only down side of doing a RFLP DNA test is the delay in getting the results back. However, most experts agree—DNA is the way to go!

Summary

It's not an accident that parents still refer to "the talk" about sex that they inevitably have with their teenagers as "the birds and the bees." Birds have a rich and varied sex life, and our hope in sharing this with you is that you will want to learn more about the fascinating breeding practices of different species of pet birds. We also hope that this chapter provides you with the information you'll need if you choose to breed him or her.

Case Studies Postscript
LIZZY

Lizzy was in luck. The consulting avian veterinarian informed Lizzy's owner that her bird's regurgitating behavior was her "normal" way of expressing affection to her chosen mate during breed-ing season and there was no reason to worry. Grossed out but re-lieved, Lizzy's owner returned home with her love-struck parrot.

AMY

Upon physical examination, the veterinarian determined that Amy's abdomen was distended with fluid. There were many possi-ble causes of Amy's condition, including egg yolk peritonitis (an inflamed abdominal cavity due to egg yolk material); pyometra (infection of the uterus); mucometra (mucous distending the uterus); cystic ovarian disease (fluid-filled cysts in the ovaries); tu-mors of the abdominal cavity; and/or heart or liver disease causing fluid buildup in the abdomen.

The veterinarian took blood tests to check for anemia, liver and kidney disease, and diabetes. They came back normal. However, the X rays showed a thickening of her bones and fluid collected in her abdomen. After the fluid was drained, she was able to breathe normally. Fluid analysis showed no sign of infection or tumor.

Since Amy had responded so well, her owner requested a pre-scription for antibiotics (enrofloxacin 10mg/kg for 14 days) and took Amy home. Thirteen days later, the owner returned because Amy was again having difficulty breathing. The fluid was drained again and the bird responded well to the treatment. The veteri-narian decided to prescribe both chemotherapy and surgery to cure Amy of her ills once and for all.

He first employed Depot Lupron (a medicine which dimin-ishes the sex hormones that stimulate the ovary) to try to suppress the ovary. Because Amy had egg yolk peritonitis, he also per-formed abdominal surgery to remove the built-up fluid and egg yolk material blocking the oviduct. Happily, Amy made a full re-covery and no longer struggled for air or suffered from loss of ap-petite. Case closed.

part two

Your Freudian Feathered Friend

CHAPTER 6

The Flock and Family Therapy

Your Bird's Role in the Family System

We think caged birds sing, when indeed they cry.
—JOHN WEBSTER, *The White Devil* (1612)

Treating our pet birds like family may partially explain why good pets go bad, but it's also how Dr. Larry's unique form of therapy works to solve pet behavior problems. Having been an animal behavior consultant for fifteen years, he is often sought out as a last resort for misbehaving pets before owners give them away or have them euthanized. To treat pet bird behavior problems, Dr. Larry has adapted the same approach he's used for more than twenty years to successfully counsel abused children, couples in marital therapy and chronically ill patients. Called Structural Family Therapy, the treatment is for people, bird, dog and cat behavioral problems and produces radical results.

Created by family therapist Salvador Minuchin, structural family therapy involves changing the organization of the family (or in this case, the "flock") and the way each of its members relate to one another. The main premise of family systems therapy is that once the hierarchy of the family group or bird flock is transformed, the relationships among its members can be changed for the better.

To fully grasp how structural family therapy can be used to successfully treat pet bird behavior problems, it will be helpful if you understand these terms:

- **Boundary**. An emotional barrier that protects and enhances the emotional and physical well-being of people (or birds).
- **Enmeshment.** A blurring of psychological boundaries.
- **Disengagement.** Psychological isolation that results from overly rigid boundaries.
- **Family structure.** The functional organization of families or flocks that determines how members are supposed to interact with one another.
- **Reframing.** Relabeling the family's description of behavior to make it more amenable to therapeutic change. For example, instead of the problem being "him" or "that bird," the whole family shares in the problem.
- **Hierarchical structure.** Family or flock functioning is based upon clear generational boundaries (or a "pecking order" if you will) in which the parents, or the bird's caretakers, maintain control and authority. You should definitely be viewed as the benevolent "flock leader" by your pet bird.
- **First-order change**. A superficial change in a system which itself stays invariant. Someone changes a habit (using

the phone) or chore (who helps Mom with the dishes on Wednesday nights) but the way the entire family or flock interacts stays the same.

- **Second-order change.** A basic change in the structure and functioning of a system. Some examples would be a change in the order and pattern of who speaks first, who is higher than whom on the perch, and an intentional swapping of roles (as in who leads and who follows).

A Human Example

Dr. Larry recently treated a family of eight: a single divorced mother with six boys and one girl. The middle boy, age ten, whom we will call Antonio, was cutting school, complaining about stomachaches, and talking back to his teachers. Once Dr. Larry met with and interviewed *all* the members of the family system, and then spent three or four sessions one-on-one with Antonio, it became quite clear what was *really* going on.

Using structural family therapy, Dr. Larry learned that Antonio's mom had been spending less and less time with him because of demands from her job and had been delegating the parenting duties to one of Antonio's older brothers. In addition, Antonio reported that he was being picked on by a peer at school who happened to be a member of a local street gang. Only when Antonio got into trouble at school by talking back to his teachers, or when he complained about his stomach, did his mother set aside the time to attend to him (negative attention is better than no attention). It was now clear to Dr. Larry that instead of Antonio being the "problem," the entire family system was the "problem."

Specifically, the *emotional boundaries* or level of relating between Antonio and his mother were too *distant* and *rigid*, leading to insufficient nurturance and support. Conversely, Antonio's emotional boundaries were overly enmeshed and intertwined with his eldest brother, who under the direction of their mother, had crossed the family's generational power boundary, and tried to act like Antonio's father. This caused Antonio to feel resentment and start acting out in order to resist his brother's authoritative manner. And finally, it became obvious that Antonio lacked the assertive communication tools to let the teachers know he was being bullied and to let his mother know how hurt he was with her spending less and less time with him.

With this information, Dr. Larry practiced structural family therapy to intervene and bring Antonio's emotional boundaries closer to his mom by having them spend more one-on-one time together, and making Antonio's boundaries with his brother more distant, thereby relieving the older brother from the task of having to parent Antonio.

To avoid reinforcing Antonio's school avoidance and stomach complaints, Dr. Larry taught Antonio how to assertively state his feelings by using "I statements" instead of "stuffing" them and then acting them out or internalizing those feelings as bodily symptoms. He also had Antonio's mom enroll him in a local karate school so he could feel more confident about defending himself from bullies. By changing the way Antonio's *entire* family related, Dr. Larry was able to successfully help Antonio stop cutting school and talking back to his teachers or brother, and to finally gain relief from his stomachaches. With these changes, the bully at Antonio's school was suspended and Antonio improved his relationship with both his brother and mother.

A Pet Example

When treating pet-related behavior problems, Dr. Larry has found that dogs, cats and birds who are dominant aggressive (guarding food, biting the hand that feeds them) or separation anxious (experiencing overwhelming anxiety whenever the owners are gone, leading to noisy or destructive behavior), come from families where the emotional boundaries are overly enmeshed and intertwined, with no clear demarcation where the person's needs end and where the pet's needs begin. This often happens when an owner overly dotes on the pet, every time the dog, cat or pet bird demands their attention.

Contrasted with this, Dr. Larry has found that dogs, cats and birds who engage in nuisance barking, meowing or screaming, or self-mutilation come from homes where the emotional boundaries between pet and caretaker are too disengaged or rigid, with not enough quality time being spent with the pet in question. This occurs most often when the pet's people spend more and more time at work or away from home.

The only effective way to correct improper pet behaviors is to make clear where the pet stands in relation to the rest of the family. The entire family must change the way they interact with their pet in order for the pet's behavior to improve.

Dr. Larry's goal as an animal behaviorist, as well as Diane's goal as a companion bird consultant and Dr. Frank's goal as a veterinarian, is to identify owners who are too enmeshed with or disengaged from their pets and then to restructure their relationships, without violence, in order to eliminate problem behaviors.

Principles of Family Therapy and Behavior Modification

There are several behavioral principles you should remember when attempting to correct your pet bird's behavior:

1. *Change how you interact with your pet bird and the timing of that interaction.* Do not look at, talk to, pet, feed, or play with your bird when it is misbehaving. If you do, you are rewarding the very misbehavior you seek to eliminate.

2. *Notice good behavior whenever it occurs, no matter how fleeting, and then look at, talk to, pet, play and feed your bird.* Your bird will learn very quickly what gets a paycheck and what gets a pink slip.

When you encourage the good actions and not the bad, your pet will misbehave less.

3. *Use positive reinforcement.* Add something rewarding or pleasant to your pet's environment to *increase* a desired behavior. For example, if you praise your child every time he picks up a toy, your child will soon learn that picking up toys is a desirable thing to do.

4. *Practice extinction.* Remove *all* positive reinforcement to *decrease,* or extinguish, an *unwanted* behavior. If you *stop* giving the student extra attention every time he talks out of turn in the classroom, or when the cockatoo screams out, then the student may finally stop talking out of turn and begin to raise his hand, and the cockatoo will stop its screaming and learn to be more quiet.

5. *Know the difference between punishment vs. discipline/ startling.* As Dr. Larry wrote in his first book, *Dogs on the Couch,* differentiating between anger-filled punishment and corrective non-violent startling techniques is important. Think of it this way: *punishment* would be if you were speeding down the interstate and the highway patrol pulls you over and shoots you! The response is excessive, doesn't really fit the crime, and doesn't allow you to learn new behaviors. Now think of *discipline/startling* as if you were speeding down the interstate and the highway patrol pulls you over and writes you a ticket and redirects you to traffic school to improve your driving. The response is a logical consequence to speeding and is appropriate. It *does* fit the crime and it *does* allow you to learn something new.

With bird behavior problems, the three best ways to modify behavior is to *positively reinforce* the behavior you **do** want when it happens, to *remove all positive reinforcement* and attention for the behavior you **don't** want when it happens, and if the behavior is dangerous or destructive, catch the animal in the act and use *discipline/startling* to non-violently interrupt the misbehavior, and after a five-minute pause, redirect the bird to what you want it to do instead.

CHAPTER 7

Jaws!

What to Do When Your Pet Bird Bites the Hand That Feeds Him

A Robin Red breast in a Cage,
Puts all Heaven in a Rage.
—WILLIAM BLAKE, "AUGURIES OF INNOCENCE"

From Diane's Case Files
CASE 1
File # 99-003320
Bird's Name: "Manson"
Species: Green-winged/blue and gold macaw hybrid
Age: 3 years
Problem/Procedure: Biting

"Manson" was a large green-winged/blue and gold macaw. She was turned into the Mollywood Parrot Adoption Center in Bellingham, Washington, because she was literally biting the hand that fed her. Every time her owners would try to feed her, she would lunge and bite their hands, causing them to drop the morsel of food.

Manson developed both *learned aggression* and *pain-induced aggression* as a result of the kids in the family teasing and baiting her with food. This caused Manson to feel highly frustrated. The task facing the adoption center was to see if they could successfully train Manson to stop biting so they would be able to place her in a new home. Manson's future literally depended on it.

CASE 2
File # 97-0055882
Bird's Name: "Leslie"
Species: Cinnamon-pied cockatiel
Age: 6 months
Problem/Procedure: Biting

"Leslie" was a well-marked cinnamon-pied hand-fed cockatiel chick that Diane had obtained for use in her breeding program. Though Leslie initially exhibited a friendly nature, she gradually became more and more aggressive as time went on. When Diane would try to change the water, Leslie would make a quarrelsome cockatiel noise and strike out with her beak, trying to peck at Diane's hand. Because of this flaw in temperament, Leslie was no longer a suitable candidate for the breeding program. Diane wound up finding her a home where she could live out her life as someone's special pet. But the question still remained: Why was Leslie striking out?

Aggression

Social psychologists have defined aggression as a purposeful behavior aimed at causing either physical or emotional pain. There are *two* general categories of aggression:

1. Hostile aggression. This is an act of aggression coming from a feeling of anger or power, aimed at inflicting pain or injury. Dogs, cats and birds that demonstrate dominance aggression are exhibiting hostile aggression.

2. Instrumental aggression. Here, the aggression may also cause injury, but the intention is to achieve a greater goal beyond causing pain or solidifying power. When exhibiting this type of aggression, animals aim to protect food sources to survive, to protect one's newborn from predators, and to keep at bay any trigger for fast movement that could lead to pain caused by an ailment related to disease or old age, and so on. Dogs, cats and birds that demonstrate fear, food-related, maternal, or pain-induced aggression are exhibiting instrumental aggression.

When people or birds commit acts of aggression, those acts increase the likelihood of further aggression being displayed in the future. It creates a snowball effect of less inhibition and an escalation in the frequency and severity of subsequent violent acts.

For both people and birds, there are several possible causes of aggressive behavior. They include *testosterone*—the male sex hormone that has been associated with increased aggression. One of the problems with aggression in birds, as opposed, for example, to dogs, is that we can't neuter the bird, thereby hormonally bringing down the concomitant aggressive impulses and territoriality associated with this sex hormone. Other causes of aggressive behavior include: *alcohol consumption or a poor diet*—if the human brain is impaired with alcohol, or the avian brain is impaired due to malnutrition caused by a poor diet, then both person and bird may act out aggressively; and *pain*—experiencing pain or being in a chronic state of discomfort. As social psychologist Elliot Aronson has written, "If an organism experiences pain and cannot flee the scene, it will almost invariably attack; this is true of rats, mice, hamsters, foxes, monkeys, crayfish, snakes, raccoons, alligators, and a host of other animals." This is true of pet birds as well. *Frustration* is another cause of aggression in both people and birds.

Being in a state of sustained frustration and not being able to fulfill one's emotional, social or physical needs (e.g., the inability to eliminate a threat or not being able to play with one's mates or not having ample food, water or cage covering to provide adequate shelter and privacy) can lead to aggression. *Social Learning and Modeling*—by witnessing our friends, family or "flock" members engaging in aggressive acts, especially if there are no negative consequences for that act—can lead people and birds to behave aggressively. Social psychologists have proven that watching violence **does** increase the likelihood and frequency of violence in children. By age twelve, an average American youngster will have witnessed more than one hundred thousand acts of violence on television. And if you have a pet bird watching television that can live up to sixty some-odd years of age, that bird may also begin to speak or behave in an aggressive or antagonistic manner.

Types of Aggression in Birds

There are several types of aggression that animals can exhibit. With dogs, there are twelve types; pet birds share seven of those twelve categories. They are:

- **Dominance aggression.** The bird sees itself as equal to or higher than the people in its "flock." Thinking that he or she is the "boss," the bird strikes out to keep lower members of the flock in line—literally enforcing a "pecking order." Frequently, overly **enmeshed emotional boundaries** between the owner and bird is the cause of this type of aggression. When owners either allow the bird to stand on top of its cage or respond to its every demand, they communicate to the bird that it is the boss and the human is an avian doormat. Such behavior can lead to a dysfunctional interaction pattern in the family system, which then triggers the bird's biting.

- **Fear aggression.** The pet bird behaves aggressively to keep those people, toys or situations it fears away from itself. As with dogs and cats, this is usually the result of either not being exposed or socialized to the feared stimuli early on as chicks, or having been traumatized in some way by the things they now fear. The same traumatic conditioning experiences involving pain that make a person afraid of birds can make a bird become aggressive and bite.
- **Food-related aggression.** As described above with "Clara-Belle" a.k.a. "Manson," the pet bird reacts aggressively when approached while eating or when its human caretaker drops food on the floor of the cage during feeding.
- **Territorial aggression.** The bird protects an inappropriate location, or protects an appropriate location, but in the wrong context or situation. With this type, the bird usually attacks anyone near its perch, water dish or seed toy.
- **Learned aggression.** Through rough play or intentional teasing, the animal learns to be aggressive. Roughhousing or teasing a pet bird can bring out aggression by causing frustration. The case of "Manson" being teased by her first family's children is a prime example of this.
- **Inter-bird or sibling aggression.** Birds in the same home fight with one another, frequently over which will be the dominant bird in the flock's pecking order. (See Chapter 9 for more information.)
- **Pain-induced aggression.** This is usually an inappropriate response due to an underlying physical condition that causes the bird pain. An example of this was when the vet examined Leslie and discovered she had suffered a serious systemic illness that had ravaged her body and caused unabated pain, thereby triggering her aggression.

Dr. Larry, Diane and Dr. Frank have found that *dominance aggression* with pet birds is rampant in families in which the emotional boundaries are too *enmeshed*—where there is no clear demarcation of authority between person and bird. In families in which the emotional boundaries are too *disengaged,* or rigid— where there's insufficient bonding and nurturing, *fear or territorial aggression* is much more common. The goal of the animal behaviorist, like the human structural family therapist, is to create change in the family system and restructure the emotional boundaries between the family and bird, in order to eliminate the biting.

These dysfunctional emotional boundaries can lead to several different scenarios in which your pet bird will bite. They include:

- **Displacement behavior.** This occurs when a bird is prohibited from following his natural instinct, such as fleeing or fighting, and compensates by acting out and biting.
- **Defending territory.** When the bird senses a threat, he will defend his territory by biting.
- **Protecting.** The bird tries to warn off his primary caretaker from other people by biting at her hand or arms as if to say, "Fly away, there's danger."
- **Sense of dominance.** In this case, the bird believes it is dominant over its person in the pecking order.
- **Social reinforcement.** Biting gets your pet bird what he wants: a dramatic response from the owner like a scream or extra attention.
- **Poor communication.** This means the bird finds itself having no ways of expressing its needs other than by acting aggressively and biting. One of the key ways for you to overcome this is to work on communication aids like teaching your bird tricks (which we cover in detail in Chapters 14 through 16). This can provide a more acceptable way of communication that doesn't require stitches or trauma to either party. By having your pet bird do a trick or series of tricks before giving it *anything* it wants, you are benevolently, without violence, reestablishing yourself as head of the "flock," and thereby decreasing dominance aggression-induced biting.

Basic Instinct:
Treating the Biting Bird

Pet birds do not regularly bite and hurt each other in the wild. They live in flocks that are committed to the welfare of all its members. Most flock communication happens with vocalizations, flashes of colorful feathers, and beak sparring that *does not harm either the aggressor or the "aggressee."* This "posturing" is similar to the wolf or dog submitting to the pack leader in response to a direct stare-down, warning snarl, or pin. Despite their formidable beaks, designed to crack nuts and chew on wood, parrots are not designed to do people harm. Unfortunately, chronically biting birds do in fact cause injury to their human caretakers. So the question arises: Is there some sort of short circuit between your biting bird's instincts and what it has learned socially? Why is it that your biting bird's etiquette flew out the window, so to speak?

Generally speaking, an instinct, like screaming and biting, is a *survival tool.* There's a reason for this behavior. When our feathered friends feel threatened, their fight or flight instinct will take over (just as yours would if you were confronted by a mugger late at night on a dark and deserted street corner). However, just as in the case of the fearful dog tied to a tree or enclosed in the car at the gas station with no avenue to defend itself, if the bird cannot flee during its fight or flight response, then that leaves the bird only one option: to fight like the dickens! However, a caged bird is not going to be able to fight effectively. It doesn't have sufficient room to do it. Hence, he may be forced to resort to a less-than-optimally programmed or instinctive behavior for its species: biting!

Pet birds, especially parrots, are among the most intelligent animals we choose to keep in captivity. Unlike dogs, who have been domesticated for centuries and who love to please their human companions, pet birds can be self-centered and cultivate behaviors that result in getting them what they want (as with most children under six years of age who appropriately demonstrate high egocentricity, and as with our cat friends, who are interdependent, being able to meet two-thirds of their needs on their own). Birds usually want food, play time and "drama" ("Hey Mom, I'm bored, make some unique sounds") from their owners. A parrot will quickly learn what provokes excitement or makes you come running. Think about it: What has your parrot trained **you** to do lately? Biting can create some great drama in the household. As with adolescents, negative attention is better than receiving no attention. And when the bird is in its cage or aviary, it begins to guard its turf, and may, like a dog or cat, start to associate the room its cage is in, or even the entire house, as an extension of its turf to defend and protect. Of course, if your bird thinks that the kitchen and den are its turf, and you think the kitchen and den are *your* turf, then there's going to be a conflict regarding whose it really is. An avian version of *West Side Story!*

My Nest Is My Castle: Treating Territorial Aggression in Pet Birds

Since we don't neuter birds, their breeding instincts tend to surface in many areas and in many ways. Unneutered animals are very territorial! Birds defend their nests, territories and mates vigorously. A nest to a wild bird is a dark hole in a tree. It can also be *any* dark enclosed space in the house. We think that only our bird's cage qualifies for this. However, other locations that your bird will associate as its nest or turf can include a box it has played in, a cupboard to crawl into, or a cabinet or desk under which it has sought refuge.

Your pet bird may bite you, even though he loves you, if you approach him in any of these locations (as with a dog guarding its bone or a cat avoiding a bath or getting "pilled"). To him, you're encroaching on his space and he may fear that you're thinking of setting up housekeeping in his "digs." Instinctively, your bird may react to this—as it would in the wild—to help its flock survive, by chasing away the animal or person posing the perceived threat.

With your commitment to your companion bird, you can indeed change his behavior, but it will require patience and consistency on your part. If your bird is biting out of *territorial aggression,* change his territory by getting another cage or moving his cage to a different location; instruct your family not to allow the parrot to perch in high locations; and never feed, water, play, talk to or let your bird out of its cage in the location of the house where the biting has mainly taken place.

The Pecking Order: Treating Dominance Aggression in Pet Birds

Birds also establish loose dominant interrelationships in their flocks. An especially aggressive bird may feel the need to occupy the "top perch" in your family—literally! If you're having problems with dominance aggression or biting with your parrot, implement the following *family rules* to reestablish dominance and make the emotional boundaries in the house less enmeshed:

- Do not hold the parrot higher than your heart. As with dogs, whoever is physically on top is *politically* on top.
- Do not let him reside in a tall cage. Again, he/she will be "taller" than you and hence will act dominant through biting.
- Do not let your bird play on top of his cage.
- When your bird is out with you, he can sit on your hand or knee, or the back of a chair only. He should always be in a "one-down" power position in the pecking order.
- If your bird has a play gym, place it on a low table and buy a model that is not tall.

Negative Attention Is Better Than No Attention: Treating Learned Aggression in Pet Birds

Children, dogs, cats and pet birds frequently misbehave because they get some sort of "payoff" for doing so. Somehow, their victims' reactions reinforce their aggressive behavior. Not backing down, not screaming and not retaliating with more violence (which, with dogs, cats and birds, is like putting kerosene on the fire—it will only serve to escalate the aggressive displays), is the key to removing *inadvertent reinforcement* for biting and changing the dysfunctional emotional boundaries in the family system.

When handling your pet bird, wrap your arm in a towel to protect your arm and ensure that your parrot gets no reaction to his bites. To "counter-condition" your bird to stop biting, but at the same time be gentle and teach it how to communicate its needs through alternative behavior (like talking or doing tricks or remaining still and quiet), you should begin with these steps:

1. When your bird has been both quiet and non-aggressive for at least thirty minutes, enter the room where the cage is in, look at the bird and greet him, and then immediately leave. Do this for ten repetitions, twice a day, for three to five days.
2. Once this stage is successful, the next baby step is to enter the room, walk by the cage and toss in a favorite food treat, saying "good" and "quiet," and then out of the room. Again, ten reps twice a day, for three to five days.
3. After this step, enter the room, go over to the cage and carefully feed your bird a food treat with non-shiny plastic tweezers coated with fruit nectar until it learns to take the food gently and without any aggressive displays. Do this two to three times a day for three to five days.
4. After the fifth day doing the previous step (which should put you at the two-week point), start handing large pieces of food by hand to the bird and praise its gentle acceptance of the food. If

necessary, use thick protective gloves that you have already gradually introduced in a positive non-threatening manner to your bird. Do this three times a day, for three to five days. Again, the treats should be small (peanut or grape size) and easily digestible.

5. After you've succeeded with the previous step, proceed to letting your bird walk onto your hand or perch safely on your covered arm (wear a thick jacket or sweater), keeping your bird **below** your chest level and away from your face at all times, while feeding it some treats and talking soothingly to it. Conclude the session by returning it to its cage with a new toy, or a different toy rotated in.

6. After four to six weeks of this, assuming there have been no aggressive displays, then you can gradually do the last exercise wearing less and less protective clothing until you are using your bare hands. Take your time and give it at least six to eight weeks.

Redirecting Behavior for the Die-Hards: Stick Training

Self-preservation is a strong instinct. If your feathered friend's behavior is not changing by week four, you may have to use a "bridging technique" to achieve your goals. With this exercise, you can redirect your bird to bite down on a stick (by offering the stick prior to the treat and/or nectar-coating the stick), as opposed to chomping on your hand. With six to eight weeks of stick training, you should notice a significant drop (at least 60–80 percent) in the intensity, frequency and severity of your pet birds' biting behavior.

Case Studies Postscript
MANSON

To learn to accept food without biting, Manson (who was renamed Clara-Belle) started a new healthy diet (addressing any nutritional causes of her aggression); received toys to play with (to solve the socialization/boredom component of her aggression); began a play and sleep schedule (reducing her frustration); and learned trick training (to establish a functional pecking order and counteract her dominance issues).

Clara-Belle loved pumpkin seeds, so these were used to train her not to bite. Over a six-month period, Clara-Belle was offered pumpkin seeds first held at a distance (in gradual "baby" steps, as outlined above). She could barely reach a treat by stretching for it, but if she tried to bite, she would fall off of her perch (a natural negative consequence to aggressive behavior). Gradually, her treat was offered to her at a closer and closer distance. Her lunges to bite did **not** result in her handler dropping the treat (extinguishing her bad behavior by not providing the payoff or response to her lunging). She was rewarded with kisses on top of her beak, her favorite praise. This training succeeded in correcting Clara-Belle's biting behavior, though volunteers did find that it was important to maintain eye contact with her to remind her who indeed was running this "flock." Clara-Belle was then successfully adopted out to a permanent new home where she became a loving member of the family. Her family knows of her past and does not reinforce the biting behavior. Clara-Belle has not resumed her biting behavior since. Case closed.

LESLIE

After Leslie had been living with her new owner, Jessica, for several months, she was rushed to the veterinary hospital with an injury. Both Diane and Jessica visited Leslie in the hospital and talked to the veterinarian, who assured them that she would heal after minor surgery. They were surprised to learn the next morning that Leslie had died during the night. The veterinarian was mystified and performed an avian autopsy. The diagnosis was *systemic gout*. Leslie's internal cavity was full of uric acid deposits, and they were concentrated around her heart. This indicated that she had been in constant and terrible pain! There was no way either owner would have known from her outward appearance that Leslie suffered from this condition, but it now offered an explanation for both her death and her biting behavior. It had been *pain-induced aggression,* secondary to an organic disease (gout) that had not been detected. Sadly, with Leslie's death, the mystery of her aggressive behavior had been solved.

CHAPTER 8

Polly Counting Sheep

Sleep Deprivation and Bad Behavior

The bluebird carries the sky on his back.
—HENRY DAVID THOREAU

From Dr. Larry's Case Files

CASE 1
File # 98-000301
Person's Name: "Ed"
Profile: Male Caucasian
Age: 28 years
Problem/Procedure: Sleep deprivation

"Ed" was a participant in a weekly therapy group that Dr. Larry was facilitating at a local counseling center. One of the biggest problems Ed was facing was *sleep deprivation*. He couldn't get to sleep, then once he did, he kept waking up throughout the night. Ed found himself becoming more and more irritable and depressed. This increased irritability was triggering his cravings for alcohol and drugs. Unless the group and Dr. Larry could help Ed cure his sleep deprivation, he would wind up either drinking or, even worse, out of feeling irritable due to the lack of sleep, getting into a fight with one his of roommates. Something had to be done and done quickly!

From Diane's Case Files
CASE 2
File # 99-000678
Bird's Name: "Tommy"
Species: Moluccan cockatoo
Age: 4 years
Problem/Procedure: Sleep deprivation and aggression

Tommy was a four-year-old Moluccan cockatoo with an "attitude," according to the woman who had turned him in to the Bird Adoption and Placement Center (BAPC) based in Placerville, California. She was Tommy's second owner in four years. She had bought him at a pet store and knew something of his history with his previous owners. Originally, he had been owned by a couple (whom we will call "Ted" and "Susan") who wound up having conflicting work schedules. Ted was a bartender who worked at night and Susan ran her own business out of the home during the day.

Tommy's first several years were spent playing and interacting with his work-at-home mom during the day. Then, at about 1:00 or 2:00 in the morning, Ted would come home from an evening of tending bar. Being able to see what was going on—and being a flock animal—Tommy wanted to come out and play with Ted. So, in the middle of the night, Ted would talk, posture and wrestle with Tommy for about an hour (thereby responding to Tommy's demand for attention, which created an enmeshed emotional boundary between Ted and Tommy in the family system). At

6:00 A.M. Susan would get up and begin working on her business chores. Tommy couldn't help but wake up when Susan—another member of his flock—was up and about. So, he too would get up and start his day when Susan did. Unfortunately, not only did this deprive Tommy of his sleep (giving him, on the average, four hours of sleep per night), but this also caused him to start showing signs of aggression toward Ted and Susan. He would swipe at Susan when she got him out of his cage and a couple of times even ran after Ted. Remember, a Moluccan cockatoo can lift every feather on his body to make himself appear bigger than normal, and in a full-out charge, this can be quite intimidating! After being bitten several times each (for more on this behavior, see Chapter 7), Susan and Ted decided to give Tommy away.

Sleep Disorders in People and Birds

A typical American who reaches seventy-five years of age will have spent twenty-five of those years asleep. When people are deprived of sleep for one hundred hours or more, they frequently end up hallucinating and experiencing bouts of paranoia. If a person remains awake for over two hundred hours, they will experience sporadic periods of what's known as "micro sleep," two- to three-second naps occurring several times per hour that are beyond their control. Both with people and birds, the body refuses to be deprived of sleep for long periods of time.

For people as well as birds, sleep fulfills *three* very important functions:

1. *Sleep restores* the body and mind after expenditure of energy, helping to eliminate waste materials and repair bodily tissues on a cellular level.
2. *Sleep is adaptive,* since it prevents the person that is sleeping from hurting himself during the night. The limb paralysis that

accompanies dream or (REM) sleep protect us from acting out our dreams in harmful or dangerous ways.

3. *Sleep is an aid to memory.* Sleep allows us to "lock in" and consolidate our long-term memories. During psychological experiments, if subjects are asked to learn information and are then deprived of sleep—particularly of REM—they have considerable difficulty recalling the material that they were asked to learn.

Sleep Disorders

There are a variety of sleep disorders that can plague *both* man and bird. For people, the American Psychiatric Association categorizes such disorders as *dyssomnias.* These include all forms of insomnia, which means the patient cannot stay asleep. Thirty to forty percent of adults experience insomnia during their lifetime. For a diagnosis of *primary insomnia,* the sleep-deprived person must cite lack of sleep as their main complaint and must have experienced this disorder for at least one month. There are two subcategories of insomnia: *sleep-onset insomnia,* which means there is a chronic difficulty in *falling* asleep, and *sleep-maintenance insomnia,* which means an inability to *stay* asleep. In our examples above, Ed and Tommy were experiencing both kinds of insomnia. This is the sleep disorder birds suffer most often.

For both people and birds, there are a variety of possible causes that can lead to sleep deprivation and insomnia. They include *psychological factors*—anxiety, depression and other dysphoric moods leading to disruption of sleep. For example, when people become clinically depressed, they often experience sleep disturbances. These disturbances often take the form of not being able to fall asleep (sleep-onset insomnia), experiencing restless sleep (sleep-maintenance insomnia) and/or chronically waking up early in the morning. Cognitive-behavioral therapists have found that once the depressed person becomes more active—especially with respect to physical exercise—they will be able to sleep better at night and experience a concomitant lift in overall mood (this is also true with respect to birds). Therapists treat depression-induced sleep problems not only through talk therapy and medication, but also by using relaxation exercises, therapeutic imagery and deep diaphragmatic breathing. Other causes of insomnia include:

- **Lifestyle routine.** Changes in normal routine, sleeping patterns, environmental temperature and mental stimulation often lead to sleep deprivation; birds, like dogs and cats, prefer "stable-sameness" in their daily routines.
- **Substance abuse or poor nutrition.** In people, ingestion of booze and street drugs, as with Ed's case, interferes with normal sleep patterns. In birds, poor nutrition (e.g., lack of Vitamin D_3), poor quality bird food or insufficient darkness and cage covers (as in Tommy's case) may lead to overexcitement or excessive hunger, thereby causing physical distress that interferes with sleep.

It is important when treating *both* people and birds who are sleep-deprived to address *all* of these possible causes. From our discussion, you can see that a sleep-deprived person or bird winds up in a debilitating downward cycle of "stress/no sleep/ more stress/more no sleep." The more stressed-out a person or bird is, the more disturbance in sleep they may experience. In people, chronic sleep deprivation will cause the adrenal glands to release the body's fight/flight stress hormones, the corticosteroids and cortisol. As a result, the mood-modulating brain chemicals called neurotransmitters (serotonin, norepinephrine and acetylcholine, for example) decrease, which causes the person to feel depressed or act out aggressively (as we saw in Ed's case). When the body is under this type of stress, its immune system weakens (creating greater susceptibility to illness) and the body increases its endorphin levels. This leads to an urge to overeat, a byproduct of sleep deprivation common in both people and birds. By addressing these medical, nutritional, environmental and behavioral causes of sleep deprivation, the human therapist, as well as the avian behaviorist, will be able to bring about a successful resolution.

The Quality and Quantity of Sleep for Birds

According to Judy Sacconago, director of the Bird Adoption and Placement Center (BAPC), sleep is as important to a pet bird's well-being as food and water. Many of our exotic birds are from regions of the planet near the equator, where days and nights are fairly constant year round. Chances are good that your companion bird's parents or grandparents lived in a rain forest. Birds are still programmed for this type of environment and schedule. This is in stark contrast to the 15,000 years dogs have been in captivity—they have had time to adapt to living with human beings!

When you take on the role of being both leader of the flock and "housing director" for your bird, there are many things to consider. Chief among them is giving your bird adequate time for deep and restful sleep. Over the years, Diane has had many inquiries from owners of "Jekyll and Hyde" cockatiels who began to bite their owners following periods of sleep deprivation. The birds would be great companions most of the day, but got testy and nippy at night. Why? Well, like the example of Dr. Larry's human client Ed, birds will begin to behave in ever-increasing bizarre and aggressive manners if they do not get sufficient sleep.

Most pet birds normally need a minimum of *twelve hours* of sleep per night. However, just because you cover your bird's cage for a twelve-hour period does not mean your bird is in fact sleeping for those twelve hours. Remember, birds are hypervigilant prey animals with limited night vision. They're vulnerable in the dark. If you think your parrot is asleep in the living room while you're up watching the late show on television, the truth is he's probably not sleeping at all. (Clue #1: When the audience laughs at a joke, you hear a perceptible laugh coming from the vicinity of your parrot's cage.)

To avoid this, many bird owners provide both a sleeping cage *and* a daytime cage for their birds. A sleeping cage should be in a room in a quiet part of the house, appropriately darkened. If you need to, put up dark sheets or blankets on spring rods over the windows when days are long in the summertime. You don't need two cages if you can roll one into a more secluded area of the house at bedtime. You might even have the luxury of having a bird room or specially equipped garage for your parrots. It is essential for you to provide your bird with not only *quantity* sleep time, but also *quality* sleep time, so take care to create a home environment and a sleep routine that will ensure both.

The Dark Side

If your evening activities are quiet, then you can put your bird to bed by simply covering him in his cage. Covers vary according to the cage size, and also according to how creative your bird is. Many birds "customize" a peephole in their cage cover (do you ever get the feeling that you're being watched?) or they will create intricate lace patterns in the cover, using their beaks. A few ingenious cockatoos even start appliqué projects, threading toys or food into their covers!

Most cage covers are made of dark material. It's important that cage covers be made of a material that *does not* unthread easily! Loops and loose threads are dangerous to active birds. These loose threads can get caught around their legs or feet—or even worse—the threads could get wrapped around their necks, which could be fatal. Household items like sheets and blankets make good cage covers, as do towels for smaller cages. Though they don't come in dark colors, the receiving blankets that many maternity wards issue make good cage covers as well, due to their soft and comforting texture.

Quality Time With Your Bird: Managing Stress and Isolation

If you end up with fewer play hours with your bird than you thought you would have, make each one count for the both of you. Be creative. Have fun. Stay consistent. Be sure he's eating a good diet and that the two of you are playing games that provide him with exercise and sufficient activity (this parallels how cognitive-behavioral therapy treats depression in sleep-deprived people).

In addition, some of your bird's waking hours should be spent *outside* soaking up the sunlight. An alternative to this for inside birds is making sure they spend some time under *full spectrum lighting*. Our normal household lighting does *not* have the same spectrum of light as sunlight. Lights such as VITA-LITE™ or OTT-LITE® brands supply the full spectrum, which will provide your bird with the necessary vitamin D_3 it needs to absorb calcium. Full spectrum light is also beneficial for people who suffer from seasonal affective disorder during the shorter days of winter. Without adequate light, people with this condition experience erratic sleep cycles and lethargic or depressive moods.

A Benefit for You Too!

None of these steps to counteract or prevent sleep deprivation in your pet bird should be construed as "bad news" for you, your family or your lifestyle. By providing your bird with a basic need like adequate sleep, you ensure his happiness, his health and your safety. If you've ever been attacked by a sleep-deprived parrot—as Ted and Susan had been by Tommy—you'll agree that implementing the suggestions in this chapter to ensure consistent, quality sleep for your pet bird is well worth the time and effort. You, your family and, most important, your pet bird will thank you.

Case Studies Postscript
ED

Over the fifteen weeks that Ed was in the counseling group, Dr. Larry had him keep a notepad and pen near his bed. Just before he went to sleep, Ed would write down all of the thoughts swirling through his head. If he awoke during the night, he would do the same thing to prevent further disruption to his sleep. Finally, Dr. Larry taught Ed how to relax with breathing exercises. Over a three-week period, Ed reported a 50 percent improvement in his sleep, and by the time he "graduated" from the group, he no longer experienced either sleep-onset or sleep-maintenance insomnia.

TOMMY

The Bird Adoption and Placement Center immediately saw a connection between Tommy's frequent sleep interruptions and his aggressive behavior. His adoptive mother changed his sleep schedule so that he had ten to twelve hours of uninterrupted sleep every night. When he was asleep, Tommy's cage was covered by a heavy blanket. "Daylight" was provided through full spectrum lighting on timers for a set number of hours each day. The result? Tommy has been in his present home for *five years, without* showing any aggressive behavior. As an adult male cockatoo, his behavior is the normal loud and rambunctious kind that large cockatoos naturally exhibit! Both the sleep deprivation and the aggressive biting that resulted from it are now gone. Case closed.

CHAPTER 9

Bird Calls

End Those Ear-Piercing Screams

I want to sing like the birds sing
not worrying about who hears
or what they think.
—RUMI

From Diane's Case Files
CASE 1
File # 98-004119
Bird's Name: "Jerry"
Species: Eleanora cockatoo
Age: 14 years
Problem/Procedure: Screaming

"Jerry" had been turned into the Mollywood Parrot Adoption Center in Bellingham, Washington, because he was what we call a "metronome screamer." For the last several years, Jerry would scream incessantly for hours at a time. He lived in a roomy cage and lived on a seed-only diet. What toys he had were hand-me-down dog toys in which he showed little or no interest. Jerry's screaming had now become intolerable: neighbors began leaving notes on his owners' door, complaining. His owners, in turn, put Jerry up for adoption. Now the center and its staff had a challenge: how to get Jerry to stop his incessant and chronic ear-piercing screams.

CASE 2
File # 99-001884
Bird's Name: "Eddie"
Species: Umbrella cockatoo
Age: 6 years
Problem/Procedure: Screaming

"Eddie" had been purchased as a companion cockatoo by the "Jackson" family in Chicago, Illinois. Eddie was four years old at the time and this was his *fifth* home! Mr. and Mrs. Jackson had made a commitment to Eddie that this would be his home forever. However, the fact that Eddie was *both* a biter and a screamer made that promise hard to keep. Whenever Eddie heard the Jacksons moving about the house, he would scream. His screaming would be constant, almost twelve hours a day! Although they loved Eddie dearly, the Jacksons decided that if they couldn't cure him of his screaming, they would be forced to give Eddie away.

Screaming:
The Human Parallel

One form of speech that *both* people and birds are capable of is screaming. Not surprisingly, most people find this behavior, whether it comes from a person or a pet bird, to be stressful and annoying. When people, dogs, cats or birds are stressed or scared, they frequently emit "alarm calls:" rapid, intense and loud vocalizations, cries or screams. Conversely, the slower, quieter and less intense the vocalizations are, the more confident or potentially assertive the person, dog, cat or bird is.

In family systems therapy, how we qualify or disqualify our words through our tone of voice and by our body language is called *meta-communicating;* literally communicating about our communications. When Dr. Larry counsels couples, he frequently observes that fighting spouses will tend to believe their partner's facial expression or tone over the words that are being said. ("He doesn't mean it. Listen to the sarcasm in his voice." Or, "She's mad. I can tell. See her right eyebrow?")

At seminars on dog behavior, Dr. Larry often demonstrates this point about meta-communication when talking about the "come" command (or "come" request, in the case of cats or birds). If you stand tall and scream: "COME HERE YOU BEAUTIFUL MUTT AND GET SOME FOOD!" your dog will flee for its life! Conversely, if you squat down and say in a soft, soothing voice: "Go. Scat, you little monster," your dog may well come up to you wagging its tail.

Be Careful What You Wish For: You May Get It!

Have you always wanted a talking bird? You probably thought it would be fun and entertaining. A pet bird's ability to speak and mimic human speech is one of the attributes that make them very attractive to their human caretakers. What other pet can literally speak our own language? However, the species of pet birds that are most inclined to talk are generally *highly vocal most of the time and have a tendency to scream—whenever they want and for as long as they desire!*

Birds in the wild tend to gather in "flocks," or groups, primarily in the morning and evening. Instead of sending e-mail or using PalmPilots™, birds will cry out over miles of rain forest to signal the start of their twice-daily gatherings. Some of their calls are *utilitarian* and some seem to cry out for pure joy in beginning or ending their day (akin to a nineteenth-century New England town crier). Some parrots may simply want to create their own "parrot music" (sorry, not available for download!).

As Dr. Larry wrote in his book *Cats on the Counter,* cats have a variety of "calls" or meows that can signify a variety of needs and/or emotional states. The same can be said for pet birds. Here are the common vocalizations you hear from pet birds:

- **Contact calls.** Birds emit these periodically throughout the day in order to stay in touch with fellow members of the flock.
- **Alarm calls.** These alert the flock when predators or trespassers infringe on the flock's turf or near the bird's nest.
- **Flirting/love calls.** The special sweet nothings members of an avian pair say to each other.
- **Tribal/flock/clan/(block-party) calls.** Flocks of birds develop a "local dialect" to communicate with their flock members. This type of language is unique to individual flocks and identifies them as a discrete group.

Too Much of a Good Thing: Ricky Martin They're Not!

Birds bond closely with their mate or flock; when it comes to pet birds, their family or owner fulfills this role. Pet birds that form a close *pair-bond* relationship with their owners may seek vocal interaction constantly, such as through the contact call described above, which their wild bird brethren use to check in or call a flock meeting. The first time you happen to stick your head into the room when your bird screams will end up reinforcing your bird's yelling behavior. From then on, whenever your bird wants you to come in, it will scream. If you scream back at him, all the better; your bird now thinks he's engaging you in a conversation—

"flock talk" if you will. As Dr. Larry wrote in his first book, *Dogs on the Couch,* whenever the owner of a nuisance-barking dog literally "barks back" to verbally reprimand their dog ("quiet!"), it ends up reinforcing the dog's barking behavior ("Arf!") What we end up with is a conversation that goes something like this: "Bark!" "Quiet!" "Bark!" "Quiet!" And on and on.

The same phenomenon can occur between you and your screaming bird. He doesn't understand what you are saying. But what he does know is that he's getting a very animated response from you every time he lets out a yell or scream. For him, it means sending out for popcorn and enjoying the show! A bird that has learned to scream incessantly will need at least six months to a year to eradicate that behavior. Invest in earplugs and get set for the long haul.

Behavior Modification for the Chronically Screaming Bird

A pet bird screaming now and then throughout the day (as with the flock "contact call" discussed above) is as normal as you or I talking now and then on the phone. A bird that screams nonstop for hours, however, is a sign that something is wrong. Here's how to attack the problem:

- **Schedule a veterinary exam.** First, have your veterinarian carry out a thorough exam, including an analysis of its droppings and blood tests to rule out any injury, disease or illness. Your bird may simply be vocalizing its pain or discomfort. If your bird checks out fine, it is time to move onto the behavioral front.

- **Lower your own physical energy level.** This suggestion is one of the ways bird behaviorists, like California parrot consultant Sally Blanchard, have taught bird owners to work with their chronically screaming birds. The most important thing is to slow down and stay calm when working with your feathered friend. Even though we know birds can do more than "mimic," they do take a lot of cues from their owners (like watching facial expressions and body language—this is the meta-communication we discussed earlier). A bird that is learning "flock behavior" from you will learn to be agitated if you act that way around him.

- **Remove all positive reinforcement.** Ignore your bird when he is screaming. Don't go running back to him; he will perceive this as a reward for his bad behavior. Don't scream back at him either. That will only reinforce the behavior and create a long-winded shouting match between you and your feathered companion. Your bird likes your being around. So, you must remove all the incidental reinforcement for your bird's screaming. When your bird screams, you must not look at it, pet it, talk to it, feed it, play with it, give it a toy, or let it in or out of its cage. Doing *any* of these things right after it screams or vocalizes will only *reinforce the behavior*. (Aha! The human member of the flock obeys! Cool!) This will also cause an "enmeshed" emotional boundary between you and your bird in the family system. Left untreated, this can cause your pet bird to become dominant and aggressive toward you or other members of your family. You must have a "zero tolerance" for *all* your bird's vocalizing. By subtly responding even to a low-level vocalization you are unwittingly training your bird to vocalize more than it needs to and thereby reinforcing the very screaming behavior that you want to discourage.
- **Praise good behavior.** Look for chances to reward "quiet behavior." Don't fall into the practice of only noticing your bird when it misbehaves. Randomly throughout the day notice when your bird is quiet. Say, "Good" and "Quiet," toss it a treat or a toy, and keep on walking. The bird will figure out what type of behavior earns a reward. Chronic screaming will decrease; quiet behavior will increase.
- **Speak softly and let the bird have its own big stick!** It is often counterintuitive for you to speak softly to a bird that is vocalizing at the top of his lungs. Those avian-

powered lungs can throw a sound for miles throughout the rain forest (or in this case, your condominium complex or neighborhood). Imagine what they do in close quarters! Speaking softly often *models* for your pet bird the kind of vocalizations that are acceptable. This will teach your bird to adjust his decibel level to yours. Diane found this out when her parrot, Aztec, was happily screaming away in the car when she had the radio blaring as she drove around town doing errands. Diane often screamed back at Aztec just to be heard! Having enough of this "heavy-metal concert," Diane started to speak softly and turned down the radio volume. Soon Aztec was "chortling" happily instead of sounding off. From avian heavy metal to fine feathered classical music in a few hundred miles!

In addition to these suggested interventions, you can employ a behavior modification procedure known as the Model/Rival Method, developed by University of Arizona Evolutionary Biologist/Psychologist Dr. Irene Pepperberg in her work with an African grey parrot named "Alex." With the Model/Rival Method, you select a person in the family to play the role of the "Model/Rival," and begin "modeling" or demonstrating with that person the desired positive quiet behavior and follow with a reward. After that, demonstrate the negative yelling behavior that you want to eliminate, followed by a punishment, so your screaming bird literally "witnesses" what gets a paycheck and what gets a pink slip.

- **Redirection: Morph screams into more pleasant vocalizations.** What if your pet bird still ends up being very vocal, but instead of screaming, he begins to sing a song, whistle or whisper? That isn't nearly as offensive to your ears as screaming is. Just as Dr. Larry wrote in his dog book about diehard digging canines being redirected to digging boxes, or in his cat book regarding clawing or aggressive cats being redirected to scratching posts or ping-pong ball chases, redirect your bird to "toning down" behavior by getting it to vocalize softer by whistling and singing.

- **Preventive distraction for your pet bird.**
  If you know that a screaming event will happen at a certain
  time, you can prevent the unwanted behavior from even occurring in the first place. For example, if your feathered companion vocalizes when you get home from work but before you
  release him from the cage, or when you're on the phone, stop
  the behavior *before* it starts. Before anything else, go and give
  your bird a treat the moment you arrive home, before it begins
  to scream. Use the "contact call" as well, talking to him from
  throughout the house, so that he feels acknowledged and secure. If you get a phone call and know your bird will try to react
  or "compete" with your conversation, give him something to
  shred or eat before you start talking. Remember, your dog, cat
  or bird thinks you're talking to it when you're on the phone;
  they hear you speaking, but can only see and smell you in the
  room. Hence, our beloved canine, feline and avian household
  members conclude we are talking to them and expect an answer in response. Redirecting your bird before you get on the
  phone to a newspaper or piece of corrugated box to peck and
  play with should help keep your pet bird busy and occupied.
  For smaller birds, you may want to use a fresh branch or sheet
  of paper to direct their attention. This serves as both a distraction and reward for your former screamer. The key here is to
  give your bird something fun to do just *before* it begins a
  screaming marathon. Behavior problems in birds (and humans)
  tend to occur in *specific places,* in *certain situations,* during *certain times of day* and with *particular people.* Use these behavioral principles to your advantage by having the bird engage in
  appropriate alternate behaviors in the locations and during the
  times of day when the screaming would most likely take place.
- **Allow natural avian expression at day-
  light and dusk.** Keep in mind that it is *natural* for birds
  to greet the day loudly and excitedly. We should all be as enthusiastic as our pet birds are in greeting a new day. Dr. Larry is re-
  minded here of the late University of Southern California

educator Dr. Leo Buscaglia, who once said that he saw life as a gift or present that we are given the moment we're born. What saddened Leo greatly was the fact that most of us come to the end of our lives—on our deathbeds—without ever having taken the ribbon off of our gift! Our pet birds serve as shining examples of how to greet each day with zest and vigor—indeed, a very valuable lesson for all of us to learn.

In the evening, pet birds naturally "call out" to gather the flock. Don't expect these avian-appropriate vocalizations to end. And you probably don't want to adopt a macaw or cockatoo if you live in an apartment complex. Given their tendency to emit powerful and far-reaching screams early in the morning, these birds could make life difficult for your nearby neighbors! The good news here is that there's no "barking" from our feathered friends during the middle of the night to disturb your fellow Homo sapien bipeds!

- **Change the ambient noise levels in your own home.** If you're the owner of a screaming pet bird, you need to meet it halfway: there's no way around it. A bird will naturally match *his* noise level to that created throughout *your* household. If you've got the stereo blasting, people talking, the blender blending and a TV blaring all at once, then you're more than likely to end up with an equally loud and noisy bird. Moving the bird to a quiet area of your home (its nest) or "toning down" the excessive noise levels of your own household activities will help you to treat your bird's screaming behavior successfully.

Case Studies Postscript
JERRY

The first thing Mollywood did was change Jerry's diet and routine. They added fruits and vegetables as a dietary supplement, and over the course of a year, he was also converted to a formulated diet for his daily meals so that he received all of the vitamins and minerals he needed to thrive nutritionally. Jerry was also given bird-appropriate toys that he could destroy, and as he reduced them to toothpicks, they were replaced with new ones. The biggest change for Jerry came when he joined the cockatoo "flock" at Mollywood. Almost immediately, as he was surrounded by his new "flock" members, he quieted down. He only occasionally let out a scream. The flock seemed to have a calming and reassuring effect on Jerry. He also made a best friend with a one-legged male Eleanora cockatoo. They played together on a tree stand outside their cages and preened each other. After two years at Mollywood, Jerry's persistent screaming behavior stopped. He now has a better diet, a regular schedule and the continual presence of a cockatiel flock of which he is a member. Case closed.

EDDIE

After talking to a cockatoo expert, Mr. and Mrs. Jackson learned that in the wild, cockatoos range over a wide area as a flock and need to "call out" to locate their fellow flock members. The cockatoo expert advised the Jacksons to choose their own phrase or flock "contact call" that they could begin using to reassure Eddie that they were "in range" and available even when they were out of his immediate sight. The Jacksons chose "Eddie, you're all right," or in lighthearted moments used "Eddie, you're all white," as the contact call for their bright white-colored cockatoo. By using these phrases that included his name, they were able to gradually curb his screaming. After six weeks of consistently using the contact call, Eddie understood that his people were around even when he couldn't see them. It's been two years since Eddie moved into his "forever home" with the Jacksons and he's still there. He only "sounds off" at normal times for a cockatoo to vocalize—in the morning and evening. His chronic screaming is now a thing of the past.

CHAPTER 10

Avian Anxiety Disorder

How to Heal Feather Plucking

'I know I swept them!' she recalled,
By rights, that bird should now be bald!
—CHARLES ALBANO, "Cycles"

From Diane's Case Files

File # 96-000456
Bird's Name: "Charlie"
Breed: Cockatiel
Age: 1 year
Problem/Procedure: Feather plucking

"Charlie" was an impulse purchase. He was intriguing because of his dark coloring, and he had an outgoing personality that won

Diane's heart. Within a short time of welcoming this male gray cockatiel into her home, she noticed that he had bare patches under his skin. Charlie seemed to be itchy and she saw him pull out all the feathers from his "knickers" as well.

Charlie went in to have a checkup at the veterinarian's office. He took a test for giardia, a parasitic disorder that frequently causes chronic infections. Charlie came out positive for giardia. He had plucked the area under his wings for so long that the feather follicles were now damaged and remained bare. Diane hoped that with treatment prescribed by the veterinarian, paired with stress-reducing behavioral techniques, Charlie would recover.

Impulse Control and Anxiety Disorders in People and Birds

As an impulse-control or anxiety disorder in birds, feather plucking has an uncanny counterpart in people. The Diagnostic and Statistical Manual-IV of the American Psychiatric Association describes trichotillomania as being the "recurrent pulling out of one's own hair that results in noticeable hair loss." The DSM-IV goes on to state that this impulse-control disorder in people frequently results in hair being plucked from the scalp, eyebrows and eyelashes. Stressful circumstances in the patient's life are the most likely triggers for this behavior. Trichotillomania clients, not unlike teenagers who cut their arms with sharp objects to obtain relief from their emotional pain, frequently experience a similar release, or sense of pleasure from pulling out their hair. This disorder, as with many impulse-control or anxiety disorders, frequently begins in childhood and gets worse through adolescence. Trichotillomania in people, like avian anxiety disorder or feather plucking in birds, tends to occur in younger members of both species and is frequently triggered or exacerbated by *unexpected* negative changes in the person's or bird's environment. Such negative changes may include a breakup or disruption in a romantic or sexual relationship, a sudden move to a new home or cage or being separated from one's family or flock. As with treating people with anxiety disorders, the treating veterinarian, behaviorist or bird consultant will need to first rule out medical causes, as well as applying desensitization techniques and making changes in the bird's physical environment, in order to eliminate the feather-plucking behavior successfully.

First Step. Rule Out the Physical: The Bird/Human Parallel

One of the first things a human therapist will do is to make sure that the client suffering trichotillomania first receives a thorough medical exam by a physician. Ruling out physical disorders like thyroid disease, adrenal disease, parasites and skin conditions is the first rule of order. Once these organic disorders are ruled out, then the therapist will help the client reduce his anxiety and delay his impulse (gaining better control) by using cognitive-behavioral therapy techniques paired with relaxation. The therapist will help the trichotillomania client become aware and modify his anxiety-producing thoughts, or cognitions, while teaching him to relax through deep diaphragmatic breathing and alternately tensing and relaxing major muscle groups. In therapy, the patient's diet, fitness and family dynamics will also be examined.

Frequently, when a person or bird suffers from an anxiety disorder, be it trichotillomania, feather plucking, or separation anxiety, the emotional *boundaries* between adolescent and parent—or in this case, bird and caretaker—are too enmeshed, creating insufficient space for the child or bird to function in a healthy way. This requires immediate intervention through family systems therapy to create more space and less dependence.

In a generalized anxiety disorder, frequently the *reverse* is true: the emotional boundaries between child and parent or bird and owner are too distant and rigid. In this case, the behaviorist must bring both bird and person closer together by scheduling more one-on-one time and reducing the bird's isolation and loneliness. By making their emotional boundaries clear, family or flock members are less likely to reinforce a child's or bird's anxious behaviors.

Feather Plucking in Birds

Feather plucking in birds is a complex behavior problem, and it can be a difficult syndrome for bird owners to face. Usually, it can be an indication of a physical disorder, a psychological problem or a *combination* of the two. You'll need to observe your bird closely, provide good medical care and then find a way to be creative in solving this behavior problem in your bird. If you're not 100 percent sure yet that your bird is plucking its feathers, it's good to be aware of the early warning signs and symptoms that may appear with this syndrome. These include:

1. Bare spots on the chest
2. Plucked areas on the back
3. Plucked areas under the wing
4. Pulled out tail feathers
5. Feathers that have been chewed and pulled out
6. A naked head
7. The body is plucked with the exception of the head
8. Open sores on the chest

Feather plucking may indicate a deadly disease, but it may also be a sign that your bird is feeling overcrowded in its current accommodations.

The Behavioral History Checklist

If you have a feather-plucking bird, it will be helpful for you to do a mental checklist regarding its pattern of behavior. For example:

- How long have you observed feather-plucking behavior?
- When did it start?
- When does it occur the most?
- What does your bird eat?
- Do you see your bird picking?
- Is she pulling out feathers, mutilating feathers or digging sores on her body?
- Is this a seasonal pattern?
- Does your bird seem to have itchy skin?
- How does she react when you see her plucking feathers?
- Where is your bird plucking? A bird can reach her chest or back. If she's missing feathers from her head, then it's someone else in the flock who is doing the plucking.
- Do you or someone in the family smoke, use sprays or chemicals in the home, or have you recently installed new carpeting, new scented candles or an air freshener? These may indicate an allergic reaction or the presence of a toxin.
- Is your bird getting a good diet? Does she eat a formulated diet supplemented with fresh foods or a homemade diet with sufficient vitamins as mentioned above?
- Do you feed your bird something other than seed?
- Are there full spectrum lights in your bird's environment?
- Has your one-on-one time with the bird changed in the last several months?

Veterinary and Medical Considerations

When you are faced with a feather-plucking bird, start your investigation with an initial *medical exam* by an avian veterinarian. Don't be concerned if your veterinarian cannot immediately find the cause of your bird's feather picking. Work as a team to resolve the problem. Your observations about your bird and her environment are key to determining her health status and in assisting the veterinarian or behaviorist in successfully treating your feather-plucking family animal. Important observations should include details about the age and history of your bird, as well as whether or not she has lived with other birds or other species of birds. Why is this important? Because certain species of birds are more prone to feather plucking than others. These include many of the sensitive, more intelligent species of the parrot family, like African parrots, cockatoos, conures and eclectus parrots.

If your companion bird has ever lived with one of these sensitive birds more likely to pluck, then she may have learned this behavior before she became your pet. You should also ask your vet to run a test for the untreatable, disfiguring disease Psittacine Beak and Feather Disease (PBFD), which causes feather abnormalities frequently leads to plucking behavior. Your veterinarian will want to know whether your bird has been in contact with other birds that could have passed this disease on to yours. Cockatoos, African grey parrots, eclectus parrots and lovebirds, for example, are more likely to contract or carry PBFD than other species.

Although feather picking can be a frustrating disorder to treat, from a veterinary perspective, there are many effective ways to provide treatment. The first thing to do is correct any dietary deficiencies by reviewing the diet and providing supplements if necessary. Birds need a full complement of vitamins, especially vitamin D_3. Then, if your veterinarian discovers any physical illness, be sure to treat it vigorously. Frequently your veterinarian will recommend blood tests to rule out all the different medical causes of feather plucking. These include:

- **Heavy metal or low-level lead poisoning.** Many times birds ingest heavy metals by chewing on the painted bars of the cage or painted toys. To avoid this, it is best to choose a stainless steel cage or aviary that does not contain any type of paint that can be chipped away by your bird.
- **Feather-follicle bacteriological infections.** Bacterial or fungal infection of the feather follicles is a common medical condition that often leads to feather plucking. This can be treated with either antibiotics or antifungal agents prescribed by your veterinarian.

There are also environmental and social causes for your bird's feather plucking, such as:

- **Environmental conditions.** Removing corncob bedding and changing the bird's environment to make it dryer, lighter, and cleaner often reduces feather plucking.
- **Boredom, loneliness and insufficient play.** Another contributing condition to feather plucking is loneliness and/or insufficient environmental stimulation, both of which reflect an overly distant or "rigid" emotional boundary between the bird and its person in the family system. It is very important to provide entertainment and companionship for your bird so that he is not lonely. Remember, your bird is a *flock animal*. And you, the bird's guardian, now serve as the primary source of social attention as "head of the flock." Talking to your bird, holding it and playing with it are good activities. This will be especially important for a bird that feather plucks as a result of a general anxiety disorder.

For birds exhibiting separation anxiety disorder (anxiety occurring *only* when the bird's "flock" is not at home), reducing the bird's overdependence on its human caretaker and making its emotional boundaries with its person less enmeshed can be accomplished by giving the bird attention *only* when it is *not* demanding it. This may help distract the bird and reduce the anxiety that may be contributing to its feather plucking. Toys also help entertain the bird. In addition, since birds can see colors as people can, many birds become quite agitated at the sight of their own blood. That can lead to a vicious cycle of the bird being anxious, plucking its feathers, seeing blood, becoming more anxious and plucking more feathers. It becomes a downward cyclical pattern of self-mutilation and anxiety-ridden behavior. To prevent this, keep mirrors away from feather pickers. Also, give the bird as much room to fly around as possible without causing any danger. Free-flight aviaries are great because they have plants that can shelter and conceal the bird and increase its feelings of security, thereby reducing its overall anxiety.

Whether your bird is plucking feathers for medical or behavioral reasons, there *are* several things you can do in order to successfully *prevent* or treat this disorder and help your fine feathered friend feel better about herself. Here are some effective steps you can take.

1. *Bathe your bird daily while her condition persists.* This will minimize bacteria and molds as well as irritants to which she is allergic. If your bird is suffering from separation anxiety, her preening following a bath will give her something to do.

2. *Don't give your bird any attention for plucking.* Don't admonish your bird to stop, say "no" or run over to distract her. It's not going to be helpful, and your attention may be exactly what she craves. This is referred to as secondarily reinforcing the misbehavior and is part of the enmeshment of the emotional boundaries between you and your bird. Remember, negative attention that causes drama is preferable to no attention at all!

3. *Give your plucking bird attention for playing quietly or for rest-*

ing peacefully. Tell her how beautiful she is in those moments, as that is behavior you want to encourage. Reinforce non-anxious behavior selectively. This helps create more "space" between the boundaries in the family system.

4. *Offer a plucking bird other outlets for constructive preening.* There are many ways you can redirect stress-related feather-plucking impulsive behaviors. Toys allow your bird to preen and act out in a healthy way, rather than turn her anxiety on herself. Peacock feathers, or something as simple as giving your bird your junk mail to peck and perforate are terrific diversions for an anxious bird.

5. *Change her toys.* If your bird's plucking has anything to do with boredom, it will be helpful to redirect, distract and occupy your socially isolated feather plucker. Break up the monotony and engage your bird in concentrated play-like activities that are incompatible with the anxiety-driven feather plucking. As we saw with people who pull out their own hair, by increasing activity we lessen depression, and by combating panic-driven cognitions, we reduce the anxiety that is fueling these impulsive hair-pulling and feather-plucking behaviors.

Sexual Frustration and Feather Plucking

It is possible that your bird is plucking due to sexual frustration, like a person with trichotillomania who has experienced a recent romantic or sexual breakup with their partner. Does your bird pluck feathers at certain times of the year? Would that be the spring and the fall? If so, you'll need to control your bird's sexual stimulation, or work with your veterinarian to administer hormone shots. Though it's possible that sexual frustration may be a reason for feather plucking in pet birds, breeding your bird is **not** the best solution to this problem. *If we breed feather-plucking par-*

rots, it results in future generations of feather-plucking parrots! We should only breed our most outstanding companion birds so that we produce healthy pet birds that are well adjusted to life as a person's companion.

Case Study Postscript
CHARLIE

It turned out that treating his infection stopped Charlie's feather plucking right away. Both Charlie's temperament and health improved with medical care. Charlie turned out to be a very intelligent cockatiel who learned to stay on a particular job-site playground when accompanying Diane to work. He would also chime his bell in enthusiastic time to classical music; one of Diane's and Charlie's favorite activities. Over a period of a couple of weeks, Charlie's feather plucking was a thing of the past. Veterinary treatment for his giardia, paired with stress-management and family therapy, had done the trick. Case closed.

CHAPTER 11

Flock Wars!

Solving Sibling Bird Rivalry

But who does hawk at eagles with a dove?
—GEORGE HERBERT (1593–1633), "The Sacrifice"

From Diane's Case Files
CASE 1
File # 99-000128
Bird's Name: "Carmen"
Species: Solomon Island eclectus
Age: 4 years
Problems/Procedure: Attacking male cage-mate

"Carmen" was initially acquired by her first owner when she was a chick to serve as a bird companion to a male eclectus named "Caesar." However, the family that adopted Carmen became chaotic when the husband and wife—Peter and Sheila—began acting hostile towards each other. Sheila was definitely on the outs with her husband and both were well on their way to a divorce. Carmen began picking on Caesar, bullying him and plucking out his feathers. This mirrored the deterioration of the marital relationship between Peter and Sheila, who were also literally "picking one another apart."

Eventually, Sheila did indeed divorce Peter. They agreed upon the customary every-other-weekend custody arrangement with the children, seeing their dad on alternate weekends and vacations. Throughout this turmoil, Carmen continued to terrorize Caesar. Eventually, Sheila had had enough of Carmen's sibling rivalry and felt it paralleled the harassment Peter had demonstrated during their contentious divorce. Sheila decided to give Carmen away and brought her to The Gabriel Foundation of Aspen, Colorado. Since then, Carmen has thrived at The Gabriel Foundation, where she gets daily attention and handling. However, as of this writing, Carmen has not yet been placed in a permanent home. One reason she hasn't been adopted yet is her propensity to engage in aggressive sibling rivalry with other pet birds.

CASE 2
File # 99-000135
Bird's Name: "Major"
Species: Moluccan cockatoo
Age: 3 years
Problem/Procedure: Sibling rivalry

"Major" had been turned into the Mollywood Parrot Adoption Center in Bellingham, Washington, when she was three years old. She enjoyed playing with a male Moluccan named Ollie, but was extremely jealous and aggressive toward her fellow cockatoos at the facility, especially other Moluccan hens. If the center staff gave one of the other cockatoos a toy that Major had recently played with, she would intimidate and bully the other bird until it relinquished the toy. Once she got it back, she would drop it out of her cage until again, a staff member picked it up, cleaned it off, and gave it to another cockatoo, thereby initiating the whole cycle of sibling rivalry all over again.

In addition to "extortion," Major also "mugged" her fellow female cockatoos, especially one named "Maple." Major would literally knock Maple off whatever perch she was sitting on—talk about birds off the perch!

The staff at Mollywood had managed to cope with this situation by allowing Major and Ollie to play on their own tree perch in a different room, separated from Maple and the other cockatoos. However, this was only a temporary measure that kept peace at the center; Major's aggression still remained a big strike against her desirability for adoption into a pet bird home. If Major's bullying ways could not be reformed, she could very well remain institutionalized for the remainder of her natural life.

Sibling Rivalry in People

In an online publication entitled "Sibling Rivalry, and Why Everyone (and Not Only Parents) Should Care About This Age-Old Problem," Dr. William Antonio Boyle writes that sibling rivalry is one of mankind's oldest problems.

The family psychologist Dr. Kevin Leman, author of *The Birth Order Book,* writes that throughout history, the firstborn son of the family is given special privileges above his younger siblings. This practice is referred to as "primogeniture." Leman further writes that sibling rivalry is most intense in a two-child family where both of the kids are boys. The rivalry frequently kicks in, according to Lehman, when the "firstborn is dethroned and suddenly has to share the summit of the mountain with little second born." Leman further relates that sibling rivalries tend to be especially heated if the siblings are close in age (within a year or two of another).

Therapists frequently use the very same family systems therapy techniques that Dr. Larry outlined in Chapter 6 of this book to treat families where sibling rivalry exists. For example, Dr. Peter Goldenthal, a Pennsylvania family psychologist, in his book *Be-*

yond Sibling Rivalry, explains that the source of sibling rivalry problems doesn't rest solely with the child. You have to look at the *entire* family to put an end to it. Often, something is out of balance in other parts of the family, usually with the relationship of the child and one or both parents. Goldenthal subscribes to the "contextual" approach to treatment, whereby the *whole family unit* is considered when a single member is acting out. Sibling rivalry experts, like Goldenthal, recommend that parents:

- Look for each child's unique abilities.
- Acknowledge each child's talents.
- Celebrate the differences in each of their kids.
- Be enthusiastic about the activities kids are enthusiastic about.
- Acknowledge their children's accomplishments *without* comparing the kids to each other.
- Try to look at situations from their child's point of view.
- Schedule regular "special time" with each child on a daily basis.
- Remember that when parents listen to their children's crying, tantrums or rage, they help them to release and resolve their conflicts and show their kids how much they love them. Listening repairs a child's sense of connection to his family.

Sibling Rivalry in Birds

If you've had dogs and cats as pets in the past, you may have kept two littermates from the same species, or one of each, a dog and cat, who were good companions for each other. When you consider how much time you spend at work and social activities, you might think that getting a bird companion for your parrot is the right thing to do. Unfortunately, it doesn't always work out that way.

Pet birds are intelligent creatures, with many learned behaviors that develop over the first year of their life. They learn to associate with a human flock and to behave like a person, even imitating our language. Your hand-fed feathered friend doesn't necessarily know he's a bird or how to relate in a birdlike way to other birds. For this reason, he might not relate to or accept another bird in your household. And, he could easily become jealous of the time you spend with a new bird. Pet birds bond closely with their mates. In your household, it may be you with whom the bird bonds.

As we've mentioned elsewhere in this book, pet birds belong to some three hundred different species. Two birds native to different continents and different environments do *not* necessarily communicate in the same way. For example, cockatoos from Indonesia raise their crests to communicate and intimidate, but Amazons from South and Central America flash colored patches on their wings and fan their tails instead, to send the same message. Pet birds can control the widening and narrowing of their pupils. Such flashing eyes may mean that something is intriguing to an African grey, but it may also signify aggression in a yellow-naped Amazon parrot. Hence, it's no wonder that parrots seldom form close bonds with other parrots in the same household.

Birds Not of a Feather

Most people with several birds have as many cages and play stands as they do parrots. Don't expect your pet birds to coexist or to play with one another. Each bird has a special and unique relationship with you, which of course can lead to jealousy among the other birds. Birds of the same species can learn to tolerate each other and become good friends. Occasionally birds of different species bond, but not normally. Since we still can't easily neuter companion birds, you'll be wise to buddy up birds of the *same sex* to minimize aggression and the impetus to breed.

Breeding behavior can certainly cause some jealousy between parrots. Male cockatoos are notorious for exhibiting violent behavior toward their mates, mutilating them viciously by ripping off their beaks. Be aware of this behavior and don't let it happen at your house!

Meet and Greet

When you first introduce two pet birds, closely supervise their behavior toward each other. Let them out of their cages and keep them away from anything that they might consider their own territory. *Do not put two pet birds on the same perch to meet each other.* Put them on *separate* perches in *neutral* territory. Then watch how the birds interact and react. Are they interested in each other, or are they aggressive or curious?

Cockatiels should meet each other this way, and eventually you should be able to house them together. Parrots in the same family of birds may get along. Conures may buddy up with macaws, cockatoos, and small African parrots.

Despite their name, lovebirds have a history of behaving violently toward one another, as do male/female pairs of cockatoos and most Amazon parrots. It is rare that birds from different families of birds will accept each other. Most likely they will exhibit some curiosity toward the new bird in the flock and come to tolerate another bird living on their own separate perch. You will need to watch their initial interactions and be aware of the dynamics of friendship in your flock if you have several pet birds.

Creating "Special Time" with Each Bird: Paralleling Child Sibling Rivalry

When your bird exhibits jealousy toward another bird, he is acting out his wish for more of your attention. And just like the recommendations we listed above for parents regarding sibling rivalry, as "leader" of the flock, you need to devote special time with each and every one of your pet birds. Perhaps one bird can shower with you, or each flock member can take turns having individual play time on a blanket with you with toys spread out on the floor. You probably know what foods each bird especially enjoys and can then find a time of the day when you can give each bird its favorite treat.

Using Jealousy to Your Advantage!

When your feathered friend sees you interact with another bird, it will exhibit jealous behavior in response, as an attention-getting maneuver. The jealous bird will vocalize, or it may flutter its wings in a stance that says "come pick me up." He may pace back and forth in his cage. If a jealous bird isn't easy to handle, or doesn't like to be scratched, or doesn't step "up" easily, you can use this very jealous behavior to teach it some commands and tricks.

For example, a pet bird may learn a new word from a rival bird if he sees the rival successfully getting your attention for saying it. He may learn to put his head down to be scratched if you groom and stroke a rival in the same manner. You can demonstrate the "up" command with another bird, so that the jealous interloper who is observing learns the command quicker and more easily.

Avoiding Inadvertent Reinforcement of Pet Bird Sibling Rivalry

If you're playing "favorites" among your pet birds, this action is not going unnoticed by the rest of the flock. Favoritism only *increases* the jealousy of a bird who wants your sole attention. You may be inadvertently encouraging the very jealousy and rivalry behavior that you are trying to eradicate. If a jealous bird consistently attacks another bird in your household, he will then continue such attacks if you don't act to discourage this behavior. He wants your attention and some social time with you. As always, negative attention is better than no attention at all. The way not to accidentally reward this rivalry behavior is to prevent your jealous bird from seeing you give attention to the other birds. Instead, give each member of your flock its own special time with you each day. And to prevent the troublemaker from attacking its sibling bird, give your jealous bird attention and play activities at other times and in other locations, out of sight of the other members of the flock. By doing this, you will go a long way in stopping your jealous bird from carrying out its attacks and at the same time, you'll preserve your relationship with each and every one of your fine feathered friends.

An Alternative for the "Only Child" Parrot: Getting Your Bird Its Own Pet

If you are concerned about your "only child" bird being lonely, there are alternatives to having to get another pet bird to keep him company. For example, you could get your bird a pet of its own. Many pet birds can be intrigued by watching a guinea pig or rat scamper around, and this will provide entertainment for him when you're not home. Obviously, you have to want such a pet and know how to take care of it as well. As wonderful as your pet bird may be, he won't be able to take care of another animal.

If another pet isn't the best option for your home, try these alternatives for entertaining your "only bird":

- Leave the radio on to provide background music.
- Place his cage near a window so he can watch birds outside.
- Let him watch TV with you.
- Give him sticks to peck.

- Change your bird's toys often, rotating different ones on different days.
- Occupy your bird's mind by teaching him words and tricks.
- Have a friend drop by to talk and play with your bird.
- Secure in its cage, take your bird to a pet day-care center so he can socialize with other birds.

Case Studies Postscript
CARMEN

After Sheila turned Carmen over to the Gabriel Foundation of Aspen, Colorado, she has continued to thrive while getting daily attention and handling. Although Carmen's aggression has subsided quite a bit, she has not yet been placed in a permanent home.

MAJOR

Major is still at Mollywood. Staff at Mollywood noticed that Major had a prima donna view of herself and displayed aggression toward females. They surrounded her with male Moluccans. When Major does display aggression toward another bird, it is handled by removing the bird to which she is aggressive and reprimanding Major verbally. She gets no other attention for her action and does not get to take over the other bird's perch or toy. Major has a special friend, Ollie, with whom she plays well. These two peaceably share a perch. Modessa is located across the room from Major, minimizing chances for aggressive behavior. This keeps peace in the household. Major has not yet been adopted to a permanent home.

CHAPTER 12

Green with Envy

What to Do When Your Bird Becomes Jealous

O Beware, my lord, of jealousy;
It is the green-ey'd monster which doth mock
The meat it feeds on.
—WILLIAM SHAKESPEARE

From Diane's Case Files
File # 99-004461
Bird's Name: "Jaguar"
Species: Blue and gold macaw
Age: 12 years
Problem/Procedure: Jealousy toward other people

When Lois and Don first purchased "Jaguar," a blue and gold macaw, he was five months old. Since Lois was a teacher at the time, she took Jaguar to preschool classrooms to both entertain and educate the children on how to properly care for pet birds. Initially, Lois allowed the children to pet Jaguar during their visits. Five years later, when Jaguar reached his sexual maturity, Lois and Don began having problems with him. Whenever anyone would walk into the room while Lois had Jaguar out of his cage, the large macaw nipped at her. This was Jaguar's way of saying, "She's mine, go away, and I'll nip at her so she can fly away with me to safety." It seems Jaguar had become quite jealous and possessive of Lois. Lois stopped taking Jaguar to classrooms for the safety of the kids. If Lois and Don couldn't "fix" Jaguar's jealous acting-out behavior, then they would have to find him a new home.

Jealousy in People and Pet Birds

Existential philosopher James Park writes that there are **three** factors that cause feelings of jealousy to arise in loving relationships. They are:

1. **Comparison.** When we start comparing ourselves to other people, we conclude that somehow we aren't "as good," or "as attractive" as the other person—somehow we don't "measure up." This negative self-image gives rise to feelings of jealousy and envy.
2. **Competition.** When we think we're in competition with someone else for our lover's affection and devotion, we will feel jealous.
3. **Fear of being replaced.** When our romantic relationship is in a "rocky" phase, or when our insecurities get the best of us, we may begin to fear that our lover is going to dump us at any moment and hence, we become possessive and jealous, so as to not lose that relationship. Pet birds frequently become agitated and jealous when they see themselves as being in competition with a "rival"—most often

a human member of the family—for their flock leader's love and attention.

Feeling possessive and jealous is more common in some relationships than in others. For example, psychologist Martin Rosenman has outlined six "styles of loving." They are: *friendship love, giving love, possessive love, practical love, game-playing love* and *erotic love.* The possessive lover, be it human or avian, is especially prone to fits of jealousy. Possessive lovers view jealousy as an integral part of being in love. Obsessed with love, they require constant attention and affection. When someone interferes with this, both the obsessive human lover and obsessive pet bird can become dangerously aggressive. In fact, jealousy has been shown to be a good predictor for later domestic violence in human relationships.

When people are jealous or commit acts of domestic violence, it is not only important to treat the offender, but the victim needs to be educated and helped as well. One of the key ways of doing this is by teaching the battered woman to look for and to recognize the *early warning signals* of brewing violence. The human victim of jealous rage, as well as the jealous bird's owner, can reduce or eliminate jealous behaviors by removing reinforcement for inappropriate possessiveness, providing consequences for aggressive acts, and by preventing enmeshed emotional boundaries with the jealous partner or bird in question. These strategies are effective in stemming both human and avian jealous behaviors.

Recognizing the Early Warning Signs: How to Read Jealousy and Body Language in Your Pet Bird

With dogs, dominance aggression is demonstrated by lip curls, growling, pursing the lips forward, and lunging or biting. With people, subtle changes in body language and muscle tension—

like exhibiting a tense jaw, feeling hot or looking flushed in the face, raising one's voice or engaging in profanity—are clear indicators that the cycle of violence has begun and that physical danger to the victim is just around the corner.

Your pet bird can severely injure and mangle your fingers during fits of jealousy, so it's important that you learn how to recognize jealous behavior before it turns into aggression and violence. Birds can't bite off fingers; they pinch and crush with those big beaks but they don't slice and dice. That's a small consolation if you bear the brunt of your bird's jealous anger. You can avoid such confrontations, or at least not "push" the issue or escalate the situation, by learning the signs your bird gives when he is upset and jealous.

For example, cockatoos have the ability to lift up every feather on their body to look "big" and menacing. Caiques get "hopping mad" and literally hop and squeak when agitated or jealous. Amazons pin their eyes and/or spread their tail feathers when they're in such a mood. This doesn't mean "come play with me!" This means, "I'm getting really worked up here and look out! I'm ready to go off!" Work with the other members of your household to understand what it is your pet bird is actually communicating through these various body language signals. Once you understand *what* is being communicated, then you can move onto the question of *how* to modify or extinguish such dangerous behavior.

There are very specific and recognizable signs that your jealous bird will exhibit when it is agitated. They include:

- **Dilated eyes.** Pet birds, such as parrots, are different from their human companions in that they can control the dilation of their eyes. It is not just a response to the amount of light in the environment. Birds dilate their eyes most often when they are excited or upset. This can happen when they are enjoying a favorite food, when talking, and when angry, jealous or preparing to bite.

- **Fanning the tail.** Many birds have the ability to fan or spread their tails wide apart. This is part of the courtship display for some parrot species, like Amazons and pionus parrots. However, outside of a courtship scenario, the widely fanned tail is a sure sign that your bird is on the war path. Look out!

- **Abrupt change in the appearance of the feathers.** Another sign to watch out for is if your bird either puffs its feathers up to appear larger than it really is, or slicks them down in a stiffly intense manner. Like a dog whose hair stands up on its back, this change in feathers could mean real trouble.

- **Snake imitation.** When your bird is agitated or jealous and feels ready to attack, he will extend his neck and open his mouth as wide as he can, in many ways resembling the offensive posture of a snake. This is definitely a warning sign you should not ignore.

- **Bluffing.** Some dogs, cats and birds will simulate a bite, or inhibit a full bite when they want to get their message across that they are upset or jealous, without pursuing a full-on attack. Macaws are famous for this "warning" behavior.

The Possessive Pet Bird

As we've mentioned earlier in Chapter 7 on treating birds that bite, pet birds cannot be safely neutered to deter aggression. That means they do exhibit behavior related to their sexuality and breeding cycles. Sexual behavior includes increased aggressiveness and jealousy, and exists to some extent among most bird species. Get to know the breeding traits of your species of bird and find out whether or not this will be an annual event at your house!

For example, Amazons parrots are likely to be "hormonal" during two months in the spring, even though they are calm throughout the rest of the year. Cockatiels and budgies are ready to breed anytime and anywhere. They're both natives of the harsh Australian desert. When conditions are right for raising young, they take advantage of the opportunity. These conditions include having a nest area, a mate, abundant food, rain to grow soft plant shoots to feed chicks, and a fifteen-hour day.

Many pet bird owners have provided most if not all of these conditions for their feathered family friend. This makes it ripe for a variety of sexual and aggressive behaviors to arise, including jealousy.

We don't understand all of the triggers that stimulate each species of bird to acquire defensive, territorial and aggressive breeding behaviors, but we see the results in our homes and on our hands. In some cases, your bird may decide that you and he are more than just friends. (Uh-oh!) If he's a hand-fed bird, he has not received parental or flock guidance about how to choose a mate. In addition, his instinct to bond with a flock and to pair up is strong. He may consider **you** as being a big bird or himself a small human, confusing your caretaking role for sexual attraction. You may have unknowingly *reinforced* this feeling in your feathered friend by giving him attention following his demonstrations of aggression and jealousy toward you and the other members of your household. When a bird develops a "mate relationship" with a human instead of a "good buddy" relationship, then they are more likely to be jealous of the attention other people show toward their owner.

When a male bird protects his "chosen" mate, he pecks at her to get away from danger and faces the danger himself. This is exactly what Jaguar did with Lois whenever another person would enter the room and interrupt what Jaguar experienced as their private visits. When your feathered friend is jealous of another person being in the room, he won't attack this person; instead, he'll nip at **you** in an effort to drive you to safety. And if you've allowed your bird to perch on your shoulder, look out! You may end up with a whole set of scars as your love-stricken bird tries to frantically peck your head off your shoulders so you can fly to the nest for safety.

How to Avoid Reinforcing
Jealous Behavior

- Don't give your pet bird boxes to play in, and discourage play in cabinets, drawers and cupboards. This way, it will not learn to guard these areas.
- If your bird is getting overly attached to you, don't overly preen, pet or groom your bird. Find other activities that your bird can enjoy without you.
- If your bird is rubbing up against you or cooing at you, reduce the amount of time and frequency you take your bird out if its cage and hold it. Remove all responses to this attached behavior by either ignoring it, by distracting your pet bird to another more appropriate replacement behavior (tricks or pecking on cage toys) that does not encourage pair bonding and jealousy.

Another "touchy" time of year for the jealous bird is the molt: sloughing off old feathers and growing new ones. This can happen twice a year, once a year, or every other year depending on the species of bird you have. It takes extra energy to grow feathers and the incoming "pin feathers" are very uncomfortable, causing many birds that are molting to become irritable, if not downright ornery! If your bird is acting up or acting depressed during his molt, supplement his diet with healthy foods, extra protein and calcium, and give him lots of space! Don't bug him, and don't test him—you won't like his reaction.

Couples Counseling for Owners
of a Jealous Bird

With the cooperation of your bird's "rival" (be it your partner, spouse or child) for your attention, it is possible to successfully stem his jealousy by reordering the emotional boundaries between you and your bird in the family system. How? First, you, as the owner, should *stop* giving affectionate cues (as we listed above) to your bird. Second, your partner should work on building a separate relationship with your bird. Dr. Larry has often seen one spouse (the one with whom the pet has bonded most closely) withdraw his/her attention for a week or so to enable the other person to phase in more of his/her attention, so the pet in question responds equally well to both partners and forms a close bond with the second person. Start slowly. Find one activity your bird likes to do, and then have your partner—his jealous "rival"—be the *only* one to engage in that activity with your pet bird. This activity may be singing in the shower. Very quickly, your previously jealous and enraged bird will no longer see your partner as a threat and view him/her instead as a buddy. As a result, your pet bird will bond with its former rival and finally accept him/her into the flock.

Case Study Postscript
JAGUAR

Lois managed Jaguar's jealousy by ignoring him. Don, the "rival," continued to take Jaguar out for special buddy-bonding play sessions. In this case, time was a factor in improving the relationship. At about ten years of age, when the worst of adolescence had passed for Jaguar, Lois could again handle him. She initially handled him in an empty room. She reinforced the "up" command, stopped giving him excessive attention and preening, and continued to have Don solidify his newly established buddy bond with Jaguar. When Diane last checked on Jaguar, his jealousy, and the related nipping, had completely stopped. The emotional boundaries between Lois and Jaguar had become firm while the boundaries between Don and Jaguar had become more pliable and close. Jaguar could stay. Case closed.

The Three Faces of Tweety

Treating Social Phobias in Birds

*Is not the sky a father and the earth a mother,
and are not all living things with feet or
wings or roots their children?*

*Give me the strength to walk the soft earth,
a relative to all that is!*
—BLACK ELK

From Diane's Case Files
CASE 1
File # 00-00994368
Bird's Name: "Suzie"

Species: Double yellow-headed Amazon
Age: 8 months
Problem/Procedure: Social phobia

"Suzie" was raised in a pet store, so she was on the receiving end of both compassion and teasing in her early years. At about eight months of age, Suzie began to react to the presence of a person near her by flinging herself against the far wall of her cage. Any stray fingers near her cage were sure to be bitten, a last-ditch way for Suzie to communicate her discomfort and to demand that people "go away now!"

Unfortunately, an inexperienced bird owner acquired Suzie and could not cope with her social phobia. The owner reluctantly turned her into the Bird Adoption and Placement Center in Dublin, California.

CASE 2
File # 99-01043301
Bird's Name: "Andy"
Species: Blue-headed pionus parrot
Age: 5 months
Problem/Procedure: Social phobia

"Andy" was raised by a nurturing, loving hand feeder and had an exceptionally friendly disposition. He and his sister, Tina, were adopted by a single woman who worked full-time. This woman, Deidre, would also take part-time jobs on the side. So the two birds were often left alone to entertain each other, especially during Andy's first year at her home. As a result, Andy had insufficient socialization with people for an entire year. This would come back to haunt Deidre later on.

After about a year, Andy's faithful companion Tina was adopted by a woman who intended to teach her tricks. She had successfully trained a male cockatiel to perform and wanted to do the same thing with a larger parrot. Unfortunately, this left Andy home alone. Add to it the fact that Deidre's social life had started to get busier and busier, leaving poor Andy to fend for himself. He became more and more isolated from social interactions. Inevitably, Andy started to exhibit extreme shyness around Deidre's friends and acquaintances when they would come over. Deidre was now faced with how to get Andy to stop being so phobic and more social.

Phobias in People

The term *phobia* comes from the Greek word *phobos,* which means "flight" or "terror." Phobias are considered anxiety disorders, characterized by a persistent anxiety that disrupts a person's, or in this case, a bird's, everyday functioning. About 6 to 8 percent of patients referred to psychologists have phobias, and about 1 percent of these patients have animal phobias.

There are *two* categories of phobias: *specific* and *social.* Specific phobias, like the fear of birds (ornithophobia), develop from frightening encounters with a bird, seeing others acting afraid of birds, and/or by specific warnings from family members about the dangerousness or unseemliness of birds—what psychologists call *information transmission.* Frequently, the ornithophobic person keeps his/her fears alive by thinking exaggerated fear-producing thoughts, or cognitions. These cognitions are frequently distorted: they lead the phobic person to *overestimate* the presence of danger and *underestimate* the availability of help.

With a social phobia, exposure to social situations that may involve public scrutiny trigger overwhelming levels of anxiety. People with a social phobia will often force themselves to endure social performance situations, but will experience intense anxiety while doing so. Social phobia usually develops during the teenage years and often follows an especially humiliating experience. Strangely enough, many celebrities and performers suffer from social phobia.

As with people who are phobic of birds, birds that are phobic of people or other birds need similar treatment. Behavior therapy or cognitive-behavioral therapy are the two most common ways therapists treat people who have phobias. For animals that have people phobias, behavior therapy is the treatment of choice.

In behavior therapy, the most widely used technique is *systematic desensitization*. With this method, the pet behaviorist gradually exposes the phobic pet bird to what it fears, first at a safe distance in its least fear-producing form—paired with treats, games and praise—and then later on in its most fear-producing form. This therapy continues until the bird is conditioned to no longer fear people and social situations. To understand more fully why this sort of treatment works, it is important to first understand how a bird's instinct as a "prey" animal can impact its social behavior.

Social Phobias in Birds

The phenomenon of social phobia in pet birds is so common that their owners often joke about it. For example, birds learn all kinds of cute expressions and tricks that they readily perform for us when we are alone with them—one on one. And frequently, we are amazed at how well behaved our bird is when we ask him to hop up into our hand and he does so without any hesitation.

However, when you invite your friends and coworkers over to see these feats for themselves, often you will find yourself ending up speechless and embarrassed. Why? Because, as your guests gather around your feathered friend's cage to witness for themselves, your pet bird just sits on his perch like a bump on a log, doing absolutely nothing. He is frozen in fear and will do *nothing* that you ask of him! As the embarrassing moments go by, he may actually turn around so his back is to you and your company. Talk about getting the hint. You play his favorite music, give him a toy to tear up, or say the words you *know* your bird can say, but all to no avail. What's a parent to do?

A Natural Reaction

You knew you weren't getting a golden retriever who loves everyone and will perform anywhere when you decided to pick a bird as your pet. You probably didn't think about the difference between having a predator (like a dog or cat) as a companion versus having a prey animal (like a pet bird or horse). It's natural for birds to be wary of new people, new surroundings, and unusual events. It's an evolutionary adaptive behavior. Why? Because as prey animals, they are literally "lunch" on the food chain for many predator species in the wild. Ignoring the warning signs of danger could mean ending up on someone's menu.

Birds are also especially equipped to react with "flight" when their instincts tell them it's time for "fight or flight." Most of our bird companions are only a generation or two removed from living in the rain forest. Their instincts are still very much intact. It takes conscientious training to show a young bird how to act in social situations without being afraid or phobic. Our companion birds find our social interactions quite unsettling.

Flockspeak: Birds of a Feather Gather Together

Birds are animals that live in flocks. Their communications and associations are built around that collective relationship. Flocks have their own regional vocalizations or "languages." Youngsters who emerge from the nest learn the flock's calls, as do older birds who join the flock later. This "flockspeak" is important to a bird. In order for pet birds to accept new people, they need to understand their language—basically, the bird needs to see what makes that person a part of the bird/human flock. A pet bird take cues from your own actions on how to behave toward a particular person or pet, because, as the owner, you are the flock leader. As such, you play an important part in raising your feathered friend to be sociable and accepting of other people and social situations in general. This "mentoring" role begins from the first day you bring your bird home.

The best thing you can do for your bird is to raise her and train her to be social with other people and pets. One way you can do this is to teach her simple commands in front of other people, and encourage her to perform these commands with them also. Allow her to take treats from friends and family; this will widen her circle of acceptable flock members. Take your pet bird to different rooms in the house and outside as well (make sure her wings are sufficiently clipped to prevent escape). If you'll be taking your bird to meetings or social gatherings, start acclimating her to the presence of a large number of people by taking her to club meetings and school classrooms when possible.

It Takes a Village: Building an Extended Flock

There are advantages for your bird to having an extended flock. When your bird has people in her life she likes and plays with, you gain potential pet sitters and maybe even bird guardians in emergencies. Pet birds live long, and it is important to socialize them early on so they will have less trouble making the transition into a new home if, God forbid, you pass on before your feathered friend does.

For a bird, it is very natural to have a large group of acquaintances. A pet bird bonds closely with a mate, but has a relationship with a flock of birds of its own kind. With companion birds, you need to find ways to re-create the flock in your home. This is essential for both play and a feeling of safety.

- Have visitors repeatedly give your bird its favorite treat.
- Model appropriate behavior by being affectionate toward your guests.

- Ask your bird to step "up" and do commands for your friends.
- Only play special games, provide special treats, or give freer roam around the room when guests or visitors are over and *never* doing these things when you are alone. Very quickly, your bird will learn that having people around is the cue for everything special in its life, and will begin to expect attention from a big flock.

By training your pet bird to perform behaviors on cue, you can guarantee that you will be able to share at least some of his intelligence and entertaining ways with friends and family. Knowing what is expected of him can give your bird confidence in front of people. Behaviors a bird can learn include verbal answers to questions, stepping up onto a stranger's arm and "parlor tricks" (see Chapter 14) like waving, opening its wings in an "eagle" imitation, or carrying props.

Case Studies Postscript
SUZIE

The adoption center placed Suzie's cage in a *low* traffic area. People who did pass her cage were instructed *not* to look at her. This created a "cooling off period" and allowed Suzie to accept people walking by her cage.

Four and a half years later, Suzie still would bite people she didn't know who stuck their hands in her cage, but she did finally bond with the couple that ran the adoption center, and became less and less fearful in social situations. She actually allowed herself to be *carried* on a perch to an outside aviary for sunbathing in the afternoon. Eventually, visitors could stop and talk to Suzie without eliciting her thrashing behavior. And, as of this writing, Suzie has become a permanent member of a new household in Placerville, California. Suzie the double yellow-headed Amazon finally obtained relief from her social phobia.

ANDY

At one particularly memorable holiday event, Andy ignored the fact that there were a dozen people at the table and flew in to join them, sampling potatoes and turkey from several members of the assemblage. His owner, Deidre, used a treat to help Andy make friends more easily. She provided her friends with walnuts to give to Andy whenever they came over for a visit. Since the bits of walnut were a treat Andy could not turn down, he readily faced his fear and would take the "peace offerings" from Deidre's friends. Slowly but surely, Andy lost his social phobia and became quite the pal to Deidre's family and friends. "Walnut Wally" was in rare form! Case closed.

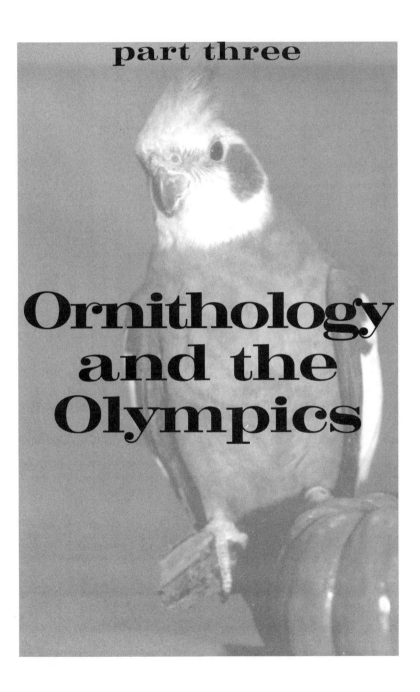

part three

Ornithology and the Olympics

CHAPTER 14

The Flight of Speech

Teaching Your Bird to Talk

I will make you brooches and toys for your delight
Of birdsong at morning and starshine at night.
—ROBERT LOUIS STEVENSON, "Songs of Travel"

From Diane's Case Files
CASE 1
File # 99-0044577
Bird's Name: "Pablo"
Species: Yellow-naped Amazon
Age: 14 years
Training Goal: Speech

"Pablo" was a fourteen-year-old yellow-naped Amazon who had belonged to one couple his whole life. Barbara and Rick were "empty nesters" who had raised their own family and now focused on Pablo with great love and admiration. Barbara hand-fed Pablo when he was young and continued to treat him like a baby, talking to him and interacting with him throughout their fourteen-year association. When his life-long family decided they wanted to spend time traveling, Pablo was placed in a new home. At first this was on a trial basis, as a visit for a day or two, then it became bird sitting for a month or two. Pablo now lives with Jean and her grown son Daniel. Jean is talkative, with a strong motherly, nurturing instinct that she has turned toward Pablo. With some practice and time, Jean hopes to get Pablo talking to her and Dan in their home, so that he recognizes them as his true flock members.

CASE 2
File # 98-0034576
Bird's Name: "Inca"
Species: Blue-headed pionus parrot
Age: 6 months
Training Goal: Speech

Diane purchased her Blue-headed pionus parrot, "Inca," as a hand-fed chick. She started repeating phrases to him right away. Every morning when she walked into the room where his cage was, she said "I love you." Throughout the day she repeated the phrase "I can talk, can you fly." After a few weeks, Inca began to gurgle when she walked into the room. This was encouraging! It sounded like Inca was making the intonation of the phrase "I love you," but not enunciating the words. She praised him profusely whenever Inca did this (rewarding successive approximations or "baby steps" toward the eventual goal), and also repeated the phrase, so he could hear how it was said. Diane hoped that with time, Inca would be able to say both phrases during their daily interactions with each other.

CASE 3
File # 99-0109570
Bird's Name: "Dan"
Species: Yellow-naped Amazon

Age: 4 years
Training Goal: Speech

"Dan" was a four-year-old yellow-naped Amazon who belonged to a retired Episcopalian priest and his wife, who spent most of their days at home. Dan had lived in a previous home where the language was—to say the least—"crude." Imagine the embarrassment experienced by Reverend Edwards and his wife, Pam, when their new bird "cussed" in front of their family or visitors from their church! Reverend Edwards and Pam did absolutely nothing to reinforce their new bird's foul language. Both of them were greatly concerned about whether or not they would be successful in getting Dan to stop using these abhorrent and offensive words.

Flight to Speech: Are You Ready?

Companion animals who speak to us in our *own* language (most often parrots) make very appealing pets. If you want to have a "talking" pet bird in your home, there are several considerations you should take into account first.

Talking birds are usually vocal birds, and they become talkers when they're owned by talkative people. Other forms of bird vocalizations include screams, whistling, singing, and begging, along with household sounds a bird might pick up, like the telephone ring or the microwave beep. If you are willing to hear your bird say "hello" as well as many other vocalizations, then you are indeed ready to be a talking pet bird owner. Some birds only learn a few words. They say those words over and over again. Over and over. Again and again and again . . .

Bird Species Renowned for Their Talking Abilities

The African grey parrot, also called a Congo grey, is well known for its ability to mimic voices and sounds accurately and clearly. A smaller African grey parrot species, the Timneh grey, is just as good a talker as its larger cousin. The yellow-naped, Panama, and double yellow-headed Amazon species are also well known for their speaking ability. Eclectus parrots and Indian ring-necked parakeets are both species of birds that can talk well. The lories pick up words quickly too, though they have a specialized liquid diet (and thus liquid droppings) so they require special cages or housing.

Though they may talk less clearly than a grey parrot, Amazon or eclectus, many of the macaws learn to talk, as do many conures. The bare-eyed and triton cockatoos are the most likely of that family to talk. Many other Amazon species learn to talk, such as the blue-fronted Amazon.

In cockatiels and budgies, it is the male who most readily learns to talk. For the larger species, either sex may talk. The poicephalus (small African parrots like the Senegal and Meyer's parrot) may talk, but their voices are not as clear as our African grey and Amazon friends. Don't be offended if you're the only one who understands your bird!

Each species of pet bird learns to talk at different rates. Cockatiel chicks have been known to make attempts at talking while still in the nest. A grey parrot may not make an effort to say words until he's almost a year old. However, most species will start talking sometime during their first year of life.

When a bird known to have the ability to talk is not yet talking, it is believed that he is observing life around him and listening. You'll need to repeat favorite phrases and words that you wish your listening pet bird to learn while he or she is in this "stealth" mode of listening, watching and learning. Some pet birds, even grey or Amazon parrots, never do use human speech to vocalize. These birds communicate in many ways, and they still can hear and respond to your words.

Teaching Your Bird to Talk

You *can* teach your bird to talk. You probably can't help but teach him to talk, if he is a vocal bird and is one of the species who learns to talk readily. Pet birds can learn "flock vocalizations" for which they are often rewarded. You may repeat "Polly wants a cracker" over and over again, for example, hoping your bird will learn eventually to say this trite phrase. Then, your bird imitates your loudest belch and you as well as the family laugh and crowd around his cage. (Bingo! Big time reinforcement!) You didn't mean to reward/reinforce your bird's behavior, but he got a loud, clear message that he can get attention from his human flock members by belching.

Birds are interested in two things: obtaining food and getting your attention. They arrange their world so that they get what they want. Pet birds notice that the telephone and microwave bring you running. Birds have essentially *two* voice boxes and can produce sounds in an incredible range. Hence, electronic tones, such as your microwave beeping or your pager going off, are *no problem* for them to reproduce. If it will bring you running a few times, then you've rewarded your bird's behavior and have reinforced him or her to beep like a microwave or ring like your pager to get you to come to its cage.

Learn from this, and when your pet bird says a word you *would* like him to say, show up, praise him, offer him a treat. Know what you're reinforcing. Make it a big deal. Your bird learns words that you express with emotion and enthusiasm. Play with the word that you want your bird to learn. Sing the word. Make the word enticing. Say it just as emphatically as any four-letter word you would say when you hit your thumb with a hammer. That will get your parrot's attention (minus the hammer).

Once More ... With Meaning

When a bird merely "parrots" a phrase, he doesn't associate any meaning with it. He is vocalizing and knows that it brings you or some other instrumental reward to him. You can teach your pet bird to say phrases that mean something in context by saying "hello" and "good-bye" when you enter or exit a room or your house. When you put your feathered friend to bed, say "night-night." Name the foods you give your bird. Remember that a parrot remembers words said with enthusiasm, so spend some time saying "apple" in many tones (this "elaborative rehearsal" is the same practice that allows people to store new information in their long-term memories). If you teach your bird words the way you would teach a child or someone just learning the language, you should get results.

Talking Back

Your pet bird will best learn to associate words with their meanings when he gets *feedback* for his efforts. Many people have budgies or cockatiels who talk, but because they don't realize their sing-song chatter is talk or can't hear a budgie's high-pitched fast rendition of a phrase, these birds aren't encouraged for their efforts.

There are a number of recorded devices designed to repeat a phrase over and over for your bird while you're out of the house. Not surprisingly, this is not particularly helpful in teaching a parrot to talk. Birds are social creatures and it is the interaction between you and your feathered friend that will help him learn, not a machine. You could use a recording as an aid, if you and your bird *both* listen to a tape and you respond to it in person with enthusiasm and reinforcement. Or you could reinforce the pronunciation of a new word by leaving a recording of your voice playing occasionally. Unless you also use the words said on a tape in person, it is not likely your bird will learn from a recording alone. Save your money and batteries.

The Bird "Police": Muting Undesirable Words

If your pet bird does speak a word or sound that is offensive (as Dan did with Reverend Edwards at the beginning of this chapter), work on muting it and changing it to something more acceptable; perhaps something that closely rhymes with the inappropriate word. For example, when your bird says the offensive word, offer a similar-sounding word to replace it (i.e., "can" or "jam" versus "damn"). If a noise is bothersome, whisper something, whistle, snap your fingers or make some other noise you'd rather hear instead of the offensive one. Your feathered friend will then learn to "bridge" or convert the offensive term to a more acceptable term that sounds the same. Voilà! Your in-laws can come over again.

The Model/Rival Method of Teaching a Bird to Talk

Dr. Irene Pepperberg achieved incredible success with Alex, an African grey parrot now considered the one of the smartest birds in the world, by developing the Model/Rival Method of teaching (see Chapter 11 for an example of how to use it). In addition, she made rewards meaningful to Alex. Instead of working for peanuts, Alex got to touch and mouth the object he was naming. Or he could ask for a treat instead. This is in contrast to previous parrot research, in which a parrot was rewarded with food that had *nothing to do with a word or phrase being taught.* Psychologists have long known that for a reinforcer to work, the subject of your study must view it as meaningful and positive.

In the Model/Rival Method, the bird and two people are present. At first, the two people have a conversation about an object. "What's this?" asks a person. The other person, who is acting as a parrot would (becoming both the model for parrot's behavior and the rival for attention) says, "Paper." The first person responds with either "yes," or "say better" or responds "no" and turns their back on the Model/Rival person. Then the first person asks Alex the same things he was just asking the Model/Rival person. This is repeated over several trials.

The social interaction between the trainer and the accomplice serving as a parrot-surrogate is critically important to the parrot's ability to learn. The parrot surrogate literally "models" the appropriate associations (word with object) and responses, and uses the parrot's interest in not being "left out" of a flock activity, or missing out on a reward, to speed up its rate of learning.

You can use the Model/Rival Method to help your parrot name things or identify colors. You can also use it, quite practically, to teach desirable behaviors and to help familiarize your parrot with a new toy or to teach him to eat a new food.

To Talk or Not to Talk?
That Is the Question

Even if you have a very intelligent pet bird who responds to you with understanding, and who knows how to ask for what he wants, the *level* of conversation you will have with your feathered friend does *not* equal that of an intelligent person (or at least the relatives we know). You won't be talking to each other in complex sentences and you won't be discussing Greek philosophy. You will be communicating, however! Even if your bird never learns to utter more than a single word of English, he will still be motivated to communicate with you. By closely observing your pet bird, you will learn what his different vocalizations and body language signals mean (remember "meta-communication" from Chapter 6?).

You will quickly come to know how your bird speaks or acts when he is hungry, thirsty, when he wants to take a shower, or when he wants to go back to his cage to rest. It doesn't take words to communicate these requests. Even a bird who is not vocalizing in English may very well understand many of the phrases you use. For any bird, whether he talks or not, do talk to him, explain things to him and respond to his communications to show that you understand. You'll be on your way to a mutually fun and fulfilling relationship with your loving feathered friend.

Case Studies Postscript
PABLO

Pablo eventually blossomed and responded to Jean's efforts in getting him to speak. Jean continues to talk to Pablo and to react to his vocalizations. He has developed whistles to call each member of his new flock at Jean's home. When Daniel starts vacuuming or mopping, Pablo says "Do a good job now, Danny!"

Pablo also calls the dog and tells her to "Stop it!" when she barks (wonder where he got that from?). A toddler recently visited Jean's home and was fascinated by this talking green bird. She stayed half the day while Mom shopped, and it turned out the fascination was mutual. Without ever having heard her name before, Pablo called her by name when she came to stand by him during the visit. See? You *can* teach an old bird new tricks! Case closed.

INCA

Eventually, Inca said both phrases. He said "I love you" to Diane the first thing in the morning. He said "I can talk" or "I can talk, can you fly?" randomly throughout the rest of the day. The phrase had no meaning for him, but he was rewarded when he said it. Inca especially liked showing off for visitors. The pionus

speaking voice is not clear or loud, but often visitors could understand this phrase and of course there was an immediate reaction
to it that reinforced Inca's behavior.

DAN

Reverend Edwards and his wife started saying hello to Dan as
they entered and left the room. For a good measure, Reverend Edwards even read the Bible out loud to Dan at least once a day. By
the end of a year, Dan had finally stopped hurling curse words and
had adopted the Golden Rule for himself and his new human
flock. Case closed.

CHAPTER 15

Avian Athletics

Teaching Your Bird to Dance and Play Basketball

Stirred for a bird,—the achieve of, the mastery of the thing!
—GERARD MANLEY HOPKINS, "The Windhover"

From Diane's Case Files

CASE 1
File # 99-1014887
Bird's Name: "Chainsaw"
Species: Maroon-bellied conure
Age: 3 years
Problem/Procedure: Redirecting aggression into activity: dance

"Chainsaw" earned his name well. He lived with a married couple, Betty and Lenny, who were starting to experience some serious ups and downs in their marriage. One morning, when Chainsaw was in one of his fiery moods, he leapt off Betty's shoulder and scurried across the floor, climbed up Lenny's pant leg to his shoulder and bit him hard on the ear! Lenny screamed and began to bleed profusely. Eventually Bonnie was able to coax Chainsaw to let go of her husband's ear and then placed him back in his cage. As you can plainly see, Chainsaw had an excess amount of pent-up energy with practically no boundaries set for him by his human flock. In addition, he was regularly out of control and out of his cage on any given day. With that much free access to walk around Betty and Lenny's home, Chainsaw began to see the entire home as an extension of his perch to defend. That was part of the reason he was behaving so aggressively.

The other part of the reason involved the family system in which Chainsaw found himself. Although Betty and Lenny had been married for well over twenty years, their relationship at the time was becoming quite rocky. And Chainsaw was sensitive enough to react to the hostility that Betty was feeling toward Lenny. Hence, another reason for the earlobe attack.

Recognizing that her own pent-up frustration toward Lenny was rubbing off on Chainsaw, Betty decided she somehow needed to redirect some of Chainsaw's energy to more constructive activities to put a stop to his aggressiveness toward Lenny. She decided to teach him to perform a variety of commands and tricks, including dancing.

CASE 2
File # 99-011328
Bird's Name: "Ollie"
Species: Yellow-naped Amazon
Age: 8 years
Problem/Procedure: Parlor trick training to redirect territoriality

No one else would have taken a chance on "Ollie," but Bernice had a way with Amazons. Ollie was being kept outside in a breeding cage. He didn't have a mate, but he held court in his cage, displaying aggression by raising the feathers under his brilliant yellow nape. He would pin his eyes voluntarily and occasionally rush at whoever came up to his enclosure. Bernice had a female Amazon at home that she had intended to be his mate. But Ollie's aggressive territorial guarding was a major concern. However, Bernice saw something in Ollie that others seemed to miss. She was determined that she would be able to handle him without triggering his territorial guarding behavior.

Repeating Natural Behaviors

Most birds are very self-centered beings when it comes to what they will do and say. Your bird likes food, socialization and enthusiastic outpourings of noise and activity. Many of the other actions and vocalizations she learns are the ones that either bring you running or result in getting food.

The behaviors a pet bird learns tend to be rewarded with lots of emotion, enthusiasm and attention. If you look at, speak to, or feed your bird when she screams, or raps on her cage, or flicks her bowl or does a head-bobbing dance, that behavior will be repeated—and repeated often. We reward a bird for her behavior by producing some kind of drama or laughter when she does something. When it comes to training birds to perform tricks like dancing, we can arm ourselves with this knowledge and encourage some very cute positive behaviors.

No Fido in the Crowd

If the only animal training you've done has been with a dog, you will *not* be prepared for working with a bird. Dogs have been domesticated for thousands of years. Most birds have *never* been "domesticated." Dogs want to please their owners, and come to consider their human companion as the leader of their pack.

Birds, on the other hand, see themselves as your *equal*. They spend a great amount of time working out ways to control *you* through their own behavior and actions. They don't work to please you. They work to get what *they* want. So, to be able to teach your bird tricks effectively you have to work at being smarter than he is. No easy task!

The Potential

Bird species have their own special behaviors that you can turn easily into tricks. For example, lories and caiques naturally hop. Cockatoos make dramatic head movements. Macaws open their wings wide. Using these species-specific behaviors, you can train your pet bird to perform a variety of tricks, including:

- Offering a foot to shake hands with you
- Raising a crest
- Spreading its wings
- Flapping its wings
- Bobbing its head
- Swinging its head from side to side
- Stomping its feet to dance
- Hopping
- Lying down on its back
- Hanging from its beak or feet from its perch or your hands

These are all simple actions that your pet bird may do naturally. Many of these behaviors, when brought together, can produce an entertaining dance step. If you've ever seen a bird show, you'll note that many of the birds in the show are performing natural behaviors. What makes it amusing is the commentary by the person putting on the show and that they do it on command or signal. Start observing your pet bird for a behavior that it performs naturally from time to time and you can turn that behavior into a fun and amusing trick.

For example, say your bird naturally bobs its head. If you can teach your pet bird to do this behavior on your cue, then your friends will finally believe how smart and talented your bird really is. How do you do this? By catching your bird in the act of head bobbing and rewarding it by praising verbally and giving it a scrumptious treat.

How to Get Started

To begin dancing lessons, you will want to set up the following:

- Set up a training area. You will have the best success with your training if you choose a relatively quiet training area, free from distractions.
- Place a T-stand on the kitchen table. You could leave your bird free on a table or countertop during training sessions, but you will have the most control and his undivided attention if he's sitting on a T-stand. A T-stand is a simple piece of speech training equipment that consists of a flat base and an upright pole with a perch fastened perpendicular to the pole. This forms a "T" shape, hence the name. You can make one easily enough at home if you or one of your family members is handy. There are also many styles available from bird supply companies, at bird stores and in bird catalogs. These range from portable stands to tall stands to tabletop versions. Some are regular play gyms, with ladders and perches of various heights and places to hang toys. These may be especially tempting; remember you want to minimize distractions!
- You will also be able to pay closer attention to your bird if he is sitting still. You will want to maintain eye contact with your bird. Many species of parrot "pin" their eyes, or rapidly dilate

their pupils when engaged or excited, so you can watch for this from a close vantage point.

- Appropriate food rewards to use as the "bridge" when your pet bird does a behavior you want to condition on command.

If you've thought hard and can't think of a treat that your pet bird likes, then you need to create a desire in your pet bird to have a treat. You can do this by offering your bird a small amount of a treat food with its *regular food* each day. The bird will begin to connect the desirability of the new treat with its regular food rations. When you can see that the bird eats the treat food *before* it eats its regular food, then you can begin to use this treat as the reinforcer for the trick training. At this point, stop offering the treat with the meals and only use it as a food reward in training sessions.

Food Rewards for Your Perfect Performer

- banana
- broccoli
- celery
- carrot
- cole slaw
- cabbage
- cantaloupe
- chopped apple
- cooked meat or baked fish
- cornflakes
- cottage cheese
- crackers
- granola
- grapes or half-grapes
- grated cheese
- half-peanuts
- hard-cooked egg
- kernels of walnut
- millet seed
- oatmeal
- papaya
- pasta: cooked or raw
- popcorn
- pumpkin seeds
- shelled sunflower seeds
- pepper flakes
- toast cubes
- toasted oat cereal
- walnuts

Training Sessions

You will want to have training sessions regularly. These can last as long as a bird stays focused on the training. That, of course, can vary. It may be as little as ten minutes or up to half an hour. You can have more than one training session in a day, if you would like to reinforce the day's lesson and progress faster. Another thing to remember during training is to *always end on a positive note!* End the session with a behavior that your parrot can do well and will earn your praise and reward.

Bird trainers use food as a reward, which is one of the two things a pet bird cares about most. For this reason, you probably want to schedule training sessions *before* feeding your feathered friend; this means he will be especially motivated to receive the treat/reward you have to offer. If you will be training in the morning, don't offer the bird its soft foods until you have worked on training. If you work in the evening, consider taking food bowls out of the cage for one to four hours before the training session. Don't starve your bird; just work around the times it is most hungry. This doesn't mean your bird will only work for food! Once your bird learns "how" to learn, he will probably pick up new trick behaviors very quickly. He may even perform them for fun. As a trainer, however, you want to be sure that your bird will perform on cue, when the show's on. Having a cue/response system for a food reward is motivating for your bird, and when it's show time, you can't wait until your bird is "in the mood" to perform.

The Audition:
Is Your Bird a Performer?

Is your bird healthy? If he is getting regular veterinary care, showers, socialization and a good diet, you probably are ready to start training. If you need to work on any of these or schedule a trip to the avian veterinarian, take care of your bird's health *before* embarking on training. If your bird is apathetic about training, consider that he may have a health problem.

Is your bird comfortable in a variety of situations? If you do indeed intend to perform on some level with your bird, you will want to start getting him used to being around people. If you will mainly show off to visitors at home, make sure your bird meets plenty of people in your home and has a chance to settle down and observe them. If possible, invite people over who have different hairstyles or unique facial accessories. Or visit a costume store or stock up on masks and props at Halloween. A well-socialized bird (just like a well-socialized dog or cat) should be exposed to hats, glasses, beards, mustaches, bald heads and jewelry—everything that is extraordinary or unique about the human appearance. You don't want your bird spooked by these things when he has to perform on cue.

The public does some interesting things when it congregates. People clap, have moments of silence, a loud speaker often comes on. So many distractions! You thought finding a training location was difficult? Another challenge is working despite the distractions out in public. Even if that "public" is in your living room, the pressure will be on.

Moving On: Cue Left...and Dance!

When you're very sure that your bird understands she will be rewarded for performing a certain action with a treat that she likes, such as bobbing her head or swinging side to side, she'll probably start performing these behaviors more and more often. Now you can start associating a verbal "cue" ("Chainsaw, do your dance") with the desired behavior.

When you see your parrot bobbing her head, or doing the step to the side swaying routine, say a word ("dance") that will be her command for this behavior, or make a hand signal for her (two fingers back and forth gesture). After consistently using the hand signal or the voice command, try asking your parrot to bob her head or swing side to side by giving her the command. If you get *any* response at all, praise her enthusiastically! She's getting the idea. Keep working on getting her response and reward her when she performs the desired behavior. This is what psychologists refer to as "shaping" the behavior. You are first shaping the head bob, then the stepping side to side and then the swaying back and forth—put it all together—and voilà, you have dancing!

Incorrect Responses: Cooperation, Not Competition

If you're getting no response or an improper response, there are ways you can correct this in your pet bird. You can turn your back on your bird (wouldn't she do that to you?) to deprive her of your attention (it is very unpleasant to be ignored or "banished" from your flock by your flock leader). You can say "no" if the answer is incorrect, although you will run the risk of your bird learning to say "no" also. But she'll probably also start to learn that this word signifies some sort of displeasure, or that something is wrong, since you always pair the "no" with turning your back or withholding the treat reward.

You can also do nothing—give no reaction. Remember our discussion on extinction in Chapter 6? Removing all rewards or attention for improper or incorrect behavior? This is it. Don't *ever* reward a wrong answer. Your bird is being "conditioned" to get a reward for doing what you *want* her to do, *when* you want her to do it.

Correct Behavior: Joining the Parrot MENSA Society

Correct responses from your pet bird may vary. You will need to have an increasingly rigorous standard for what you consider to be a "correct" behavioral response in order to acknowledge your parrot and reward her. Your bird's first attempts to do the behavior might be tentative. Great! That's a big deal, that's a four-toed step in the right direction. Reward your bird with praise and a treat. But, try to avoid consistently cuing your bird to do the behavior badly; you don't want to settle for a low level of performance. Ratchet up the level of excellence that you'll accept. Start *only* rewarding the bird that produces a more enthusiastic and deeper head bob or leg dance. And so on and so on. Work slowly toward your *ideal level of correct performance* and let the parrot know what you are aiming for. Bob your own head to show her if you need to. You can keep raising the standards of what will earn a food reward and praise until your parrot performs the behavior at the highest level of desired competency.

If you're working with a parrot that already has some repertoire of tricks, you will want to reward her for *only* doing the behavior that you want at the time—not haphazardly performing her whole briefcase full of tricks. If she does other behaviors not related to the trick you are cuing her for, say dancing side to side, then don't reward her. You are training her to respond to *your* cues, after all, not to be a showoff. Chances are that your trained bird will be trying out all sorts of behavior to see what exactly it takes to elicit that much desired, but frequently elusive reward.

The "Larry Bird" of Birds:
Teaching Your Bird to
Play Basketball!

Start training simple behaviors. If you want your pet bird to perform a complex trick, such as teaching your bird to put a ball in a basket, you will need to break it down into several smaller behaviors. Basically, putting a ball in a basket is a "retrieve" maneuver where the bird does not return the ball to you, but drops it in a receptacle that you designate.

In your first couple of sessions, you will introduce your feathered friend to the ball. An appropriately sized ball with holes in it will be easiest for your bird to carry. Observe both the bird and ball on a flat surface. If your bird touches the ball at all, use your bridge, make your hand signal and praise your bird profusely. Reward him for touching the ball. In subsequent lessons, reward him for picking up the ball. Once your bird knows how to pick up and carry the ball, you are ready to work on the retrieve command.

Ask your bird to bring the ball to you. If you need to, guide your bird with your hand and show him what you want. Praise him for heading in your direction, then for coming to you and giving you the ball. Then ask him to drop the ball in your hand or on the table. You can hold a favorite treat in your hand to entice him to drop the ball when he gets to you. In order to eat the treat, he'll have to relinquish the object upon hearing "drop."

Once your pet bird is bringing the ball to you and dropping it in your hand, ask him to drop the ball into a basket that can be used for a parrot-sized basketball hoop. Hold the hoop at the end of the table, with the basket at your bird's level. Remember to cue your bird to do his behavior, and to praise him profusely when he does it right. You can say "no" or turn your back when he is not performing correctly.

Gradually, raise the basket at the side of the table. Eventually your feathered friend will have to reach up and drop his ball in the hoop. Congratulations—you've learned a parlor trick! Avian aerobic basketball! Harlem Globetrotters—watch out!

Many other tricks are based on the "bring it to me" cue or "fetch" command. Your bird can learn to pull a wagon or push a cart in the very same manner as described here.

Opening Night: The End Result

By trick training your pet bird, you have opened up a very special line of communication between the two of you. She can now learn ways to get treats and attention from you—her flock leader. Not a bad thing! That's the motivating factor for your bird. On the flip side, you are learning how to teach your bird to do something, which requires you to observe her more closely than you would normally. It raises the level and quality of your interaction beyond the customary pet/owner relationship. Your bird feels valued and now has a job to do in the flock and for the flock leader. In addition, with success at training, you get some of that praise and reward coming back at you from the impressed reactions of your family and friends. A win-win-win situation for the entire flock.

The Pet Human

Your bird may have you pretty well trained now to provide him with attention, snacks and entertainment. You're going to have to turn the tables on him and train your bird to do something that pleases *you* instead. This mind-set will serve you well, and will help to make training your bird fun.

The other essential quality you will need plenty of in training sessions is patience. You will be doing lessons over and over. You will be waiting for your bird to respond. You will repeat commands. There will be days when your bird is not interested. There will be days when you are not interested in training. There will also be breakthrough moments when your bird understands exactly what you are trying to do and starts to work with you.

Besides patience, patience and more patience, you will also need to keep your sense of humor. You will need to train your bird at least daily up to two or three short sessions per day. Things will sometimes go well and sometimes they won't. If you can keep your sense of humor, have fun and enjoy interacting with your bird, then it will all be worthwhile. Even if you're never on center stage at a theme park, you've crossed the line into some interspecies communication that will enrich you and your pet bird's lives forever.

Case Studies Postscript
CHAINSAW

Betty started to teach Chainsaw tricks. Eventually, she was able to have Chainsaw perform these feats for friends and neighbors. He even put in an appearance at the local bird club.

In redirecting Chainsaw's pent-up energy by teaching him to dance, stand on his head and to come on request, Betty gained a more peaceful home environment. Chainsaw enjoyed his training lessons immensely and now had constructive ways in which to elicit attention from his family members. And he never bit Lenny on the ear again.

OLLIE

Bernice began by introducing Ollie to a more healthy diet consisting of fresh-sprouted seed and additional nutrients and vitamins supplements. Ollie began to live in the house and became familiar with Bernice and her family's routine. He was eventually allowed out of his cage, and could observe the interaction between Bernice and the other parrots. Gradually, Ollie started to approach and step up to Bernice's hand. He eventually progressed to the point that she could hold him on his back in her palm.

Ollie had a natural tendency to grab at something when he was on his back. So, Bernice took advantage of this trait and began offering Ollie his own tail feathers to hold on to. He began to fan and hold open his tail on command as his first trick. Ollie also learned to wave one of his feet in a very cute and distinct manner. Ollie was now responsive enough to Bernice and no longer excessively territorial so he could begin serving his duty as a breeding bird. Bernice even got to the point of being able to reach into Ollie's nest to check on eggs or chicks, and could now easily handle Ollie outside of his cage—even in the middle of the breeding season! By teaching Ollie the parlor trick of stepping up to her hand and fanning and holding his tail while lying on his back, Bernice had built a mutually trusting relationship with Ollie, which helped him drop his protective instincts about his cage, his perch and his own bird family.

CHAPTER 16

Lassie, Come Home!

Teaching Your Bird Commands

If you cannot catch the bird of paradise,
better take a wet hen.
—NIKITA KHRUSHCHEV

From Diane's Case Files
File # 98-0466990
Bird's Name: "Boris"
Species: Cockatiel
Age: 2 years
Problem/Procedure: Learning to come on command

"Boris" was two years old when Diane met him. Boris needed a home, and was placed with a Silicon Valley engineer named Sam. Sam had just gotten divorced and was building a new life for himself. He enjoyed his bird's company and spent quite a bit of time with him. But Sam wanted to do more. Since Boris was so tame, Sam wanted to deepen their connection by teaching him some basic commands. Could he teach Boris to "come" on command?

Making Life Easier

Your pet bird is well adapted to living in the rain forest or a grassy savannah, and her parents or grandparents most likely were living in their native habitat. Therefore, she will require some training in the skills that make her a good household companion for a human being.

One of the fundamental commands to teach your feathered friend is the "up" command. This is actually the first step to eventually teaching your pet bird to "come" on command. One of the consistent reasons pet birds are not reunited with their homes when they accidentally get loose outside is that *they do not know how to return to their owner or come on command.* By practicing the "come" command as outlined below, you reduce the chance, that in an emergency, your bird will fly off (akin to a dog running out the front door) and lose its bearings, never to return to you and its flock again.

Dogs and Birds

When Dr. Larry lectures on the "come" command for dogs, he lists four instances where an owner should *never* use that command. They are:

- For punishment
- For grooming or medical care
- For isolation or being penned up

- For calling the dog out of the comfortable shade into the blistering heat of the sun.

If dog owners do in fact call their dogs to come for any of these four instances, they will be actively teaching their dogs to *never* come to them again. The dog learns that "come" equals bad things: punishment, painful grooming, isolation from the pack and/or french-frying in the sun!

Well, the same applies to your pet bird. Be careful to *not* use the "come" command for something negative from your bird's point of view. Or else, like the uninformed dog owner, you will be teaching your bird to literally head for the trees when he hears you use that word.

Breaking Down the "Come" Command into Steps: Teaching the "Up" Command First

You can teach your pet bird the "up" command in a single lesson. After that initial lesson, practice until the command becomes automatic. When a bird is going through avian adolescence, it might not listen to you or will test your dominance (as your teenaged kids once did). Then you'll need to go through the same training again as a reminder.

To teach the "up" command, do the following steps:

- Work with your feathered friend in a room or space where she cannot see or get to her cage.
- Let her down on a surface, even on the floor.
- Use one hand to guide your bird from behind.
- Press an index finger into the bird's chest above her feet.
- Push her up gently from behind to start working on the "up" command.

- Now, start a ladder of "up" commands over and over. Show your parrot what you expect of her.
- Once she's on one of your index fingers, rotate that finger backwards slowly to unbalance your parrot.
- At the same time, push the index finger of your other hand up onto your bird's chest above her feet. She'll sense there's somewhere steady to go and will step up onto the next finger held out to her.
- Say "up" as your pet bird is stepping onto the new finger. A parrot will want to get up off the floor and onto a higher perch.
- You can give her that security by practicing "up" commands that get her progressively higher till you're looking each other in the face. Start "up" commands at the floor whenever your bird flies off a perch or hand.
- Keep repeating this, saying "up" consistently as your bird steps onto your finger.
- Add "down" when she steps off your hand onto her cage or a perch.
- After a few tries, your bird should be raising her foot to step up or following the command on her own. Practice until your feathered friend knows that "up" is a command she responds to consistently. Don't let her *not* step up once you've asked her to. If she just sits there, use both hands and guide her up onto your hand or finger. Praise her profusely for her actions.

A bird will learn to respond to any spoken, whistled, verbalized or signaled command you choose to signify "step up." The command "up" has become conventional, though, and will be less confusing to other companion bird lovers.

Come, Polly, Come!

You can teach your feathered friend to "come" once she knows the "up" command. Here's what to do:

- Move your finger a short distance from your bird, and ask her to step "up." She should hop onto your finger. Praise her.
- A dog is excited about coming and about pleasing you by doing so. Birds are more deliberate in their actions. Your bird may react slowly or think about taking a leap to your finger. Praise any motion in the desired direction and be patient!
- Gradually move your finger farther. A bird that can fly will learn to fly to you this way. If your parrot has clipped wings, be sure she can walk across the table or floor to you.
- When you practice, also ask your bird to come down to you. Many escaped birds don't know how to get down from heights. Have your feathered friend climb down curtains to you, as well as waddle across the floor.
- If you want, add a hand signal as well as a voice command to this behavior. A bird has excellent eyesight and will catch your hand signal from quite a distance.
- When your bird comes to you when asked, praise her.
- If she is outside or in danger and you call her, *don't scold her after she comes to you.* Only praise her for coming, not for flying away or getting into trouble, so that you don't end up sending mixed messages! (Remember Dr. Larry's parallel instruction for dog owners cited above.)

Practical Maneuvers

Once your pet bird knows how to get on your finger when you say "up," then you're ready to continue to teach her to be a respectable member of a human flock. If your bird didn't come with the skill of quietly entering and exiting her cage, that's a good skill to work on now.

- Start with the bird out of the cage.
- Review the "up" command a couple times.
- Now, with your bird on your finger, hold her close to the cage

door, then bring her back to you and go on playing outside the cage.

- Tell her what a good girl she is. Teach the whole behavior in steps. Do this first step for several days to a week, merely getting your bird close to the cage.
- Next, with your bird still on your finger, put her into and out of the cage calmly. Do this for a few days to a week till she gets used to this new development (akin to getting a dog used to going through his dog door).
- In the next step, have your bird get off onto a perch inside the cage, then immediately ask her to step back "up" onto your finger and exit the cage with her on your finger. Now practice this step. You're teaching your bird to get onto your finger, to leave the cage, and to enter it quietly.
- The last step is to go ahead and try calmly putting your hand into your bird's cage, and ask her to step "up" so that she can come out of the cage. If she isn't ready yet, go back to earlier behaviors and keep working on them before trying the "up" command inside her cage. A pet bird's cage is her private space. It's a big deal for her to allow you to invade her space and to take her out of a secure space. It's well worth working on perfecting an easy exit, however.

Leaving for Work

Another behavior that makes birds into better citizens is teaching them how to go back into their cages quietly. You know how harried you can be in the morning when you're leaving for work or you're late for an appointment. Your pet bird will sense the hurried energy and will stay out of your frantic grasp as you prepare to exit the premises. *The best thing you can do is to calm down.* The next thing that will help you is the judicious use of the "up" command (but not the "come" command). Get your bird on your finger or hand. Then restrain your feathered friend so the comedy doesn't start over again. Hold your hands over her wings, or clamp your thumb over her feet to keep her from leaving you. You probably need to gradually work up to either method of restraint, first by just touching your parrot on her back or feet, and gradually applying more pressure. Make sure lots of delicious treats are awaiting your bird once she is returned to her cage, which will make this a positive experience.

Playing Alone Quietly

It's important to teach a pet bird to play alone quietly. When you first bring your bird home, you and your pet will be enthralled with one another and you may want to spend a great deal of time with her. Realistically, however, your normal routine will not be bird-centered. If your bird knows how to play with toys and keep herself entertained in your absence, then you'll have a much better relationship.

Your bird can learn to stay on a play gym, cage top or in a designated play area. Be persistent about this rule and *don't allow your parrot to have the run of the house* (remember the case of "Chainsaw," in an earlier chapter?). This is especially important for a territorial or a manipulative bird. *They need boundaries in their lives.* Whenever your bird leaves the designated play area, put her back. Over and over again. Eventually she'll give up trying to leave, and should give up trying to defend the huge territory of the entire house. Of course, your bird will test your rule every so often, so you need to uphold it consistently.

The Avian Toy Chest

Expose your pet bird early and often to the joys of playing with toys. Buy a variety of toys suitable for your feathered friend, and turn everyday items into toys. Shop at garage sales for clean, safe human baby toys. Toys keep a bird entertained. Use your bird's natural penchant for picking things up and chewing, as well as his fascination with colors to keep him entertained. Let him chew up mail you don't want to save, string Cheerios on a shoelace, roll a bottle cap around or pick at a new Kleenex box. A busy bird is a happy bird.

The Adaptable Bird

Pet birds can get stuck in a rut easily (as do dogs and cats who prefer "stable-sameness" in their routines). Exposing your bird to a variety of situations and to a variety of people will help him to be more socially adjusted and accept new things as they come along. You can do this in a simple way: by making it a practice to take your bird with you into different rooms of your house. He'll get used to the variety of wall décor and furniture that way. Take him in or out of his cage. You can even set up bird playgrounds in each room, so he can be with you if you have a reason to stay there for a while.

Introduce your pet bird to your friends and family. Teach her to step off your hand onto someone else's hand if you request it and to be polite about it! *Only allow your bird to socialize like this if your bird is trustworthy and not apt to bite.* If your bird might bite, then take charge and set the rules for interaction between your bird and visitors. Remember that not everyone knows about birds. Show your friends how to pet your bird and remind them she likes shiny objects, so they don't get tugged by the earring or lose a precious stone from a precious ring. There's something fascinating about glasses, too. People with glasses who meet a curious and outgoing bird are likely to end up with a bird dangling from their frame. You be the judge of your friend's tolerance and control the situation so it doesn't get out of hand!

You can extend your bird's socialization by taking him to meetings or gatherings. Ask for permission. It is fine to take a bird to some classrooms and some bird club meetings.

Working with a Pet Bird Behaviorist

If you want to go beyond the "up" and "come" commands in shaping your bird's behavior, you might want to hire a professional. There are people who specialize in working with birds and their families to modify behavior so that a household is more peaceful. The earlier you get this kind of help, the easier it will be to modify offending behaviors. A pet bird behaviorist may consult with you in person or on the phone. The behaviorist will ask you many questions about the problems you are having with your bird, her routine, and relationships among the inhabitants of the household. A behaviorist who visits you in your home will observe the environment in which your bird lives. Often, a behaviorist can show you handling techniques that improve the relationship between you and your bird. Obviously, calling in an expert at the first sign of trouble can save you and your bird a lot of grief.

However, modifying a behavior in your bird is not a quick fix. Expect to spend several weeks to months gradually modifying an unwanted behavior. It's up to you to use the advice you are given and apply it consistently for both you and your bird. Your bird and the rest of your "flock" will thank you.

Case Study Postscript
BORIS

Sam began to whistle every time Boris stepped on his finger. On a lark, he started asking him to "come" from greater and greater distances when he whistled. Eventually, Boris literally flew across the room to get to Sam no matter where he was in the house. Boris enjoyed his "come" command and Sam enjoyed showing his "Lassie Bird" off to friends. Transition successful. Case closed.

Appendix A

Bird and Veterinary Organizations*

ACADEMY OF VETERINARY
HOMEOPATHY (AVH)
751 N.E. 168th Street
North Miami, FL 33162-2427
(305) 652-1590
FX (305) 653-7244
Email: *webmaster@theavh.org*
Web: *http://www.acadvethom.org*

AFRICAN PARROT SOCIETY (APS)
P.O. Box 204
Clarinda, IA 51632
(712) 542-4190
FX (712) 542-6208
Email:
Randyk@clarinda.heartland.net
Web: *http://www.wingscc.com/aps*

AMAZON SOCIETY (AS)
C/O Diana M. Holloway,
President
235 North Walnut Street
Bryan, OH 43506
(419) 636-3882
Email: *Holloway@saa.net*
Web: *http://www.upatsix.com/
amazona*

AMERICAN ACADEMY OF VETERINARY
DERMATOLOGY (AAVD)
C/O Dr. Nita Gulbas
Desert Sage Veterinary Clinic
2249 W. Bethany Home Road
Phoenix, AZ 85015
(602) 433-0198
FX (602) 336-0146

AMERICAN ACADEMY OF
VETERINARY PHARMACOLOGY &
THERAPEUTICS (AAVPT)
Department of Veterinary
Biosciences
University of Illinois
2001 S. Lincoln Avenue
Urbana, IL 61801
Dr. Jean Powers, Secretary-
Treasurer
(217) 333-7981

AMERICAN ANIMAL HOSPITAL
ASSOCIATION (AAHA)
P.O. Box 150899
Denver, CO 80215-0899
John W. Albers, DVM, Executive
Director
(303) 986-2800
Email: *aahapr@aol.com*
Web: *http://www.healthypet.com*

*Alphabetically by name of the organization.

AMERICAN ASSOCIATION OF AVIAN
  PATHOLOGISTS (AAAP)
University of Pennsylvania
New Bolton Center
Kennett Square, PA 19348
Dr. Robert J. Eckroade,
Secretary-Treasurer
(610) 444-4282
FX (610) 925-8106
Email: *aaap@vet.upenn.edu*

AMERICAN ASSOCIATION OF
  VETERINARY IMMUNOLOGISTS
  (AAVI)
USDA
ARS
337 Bustad Hall
Washington State University
Pullman, WA 99164-7030
Dr. Will Goff, Secretary-Treasurer
(509) 335-6029
Email: *wgoff@vetmed.wsu.edu*
Web:
*http://hsc.missouri.edu/vetmed/aari/
docs/aarihome.html*

AMERICAN ASSOCIATION OF
  VETERINARY LABORATORY
  DIAGNOSTICIANS (AAVLD)
University of California—Davis
P.O. Box 1522
Turlock, CA 95381
Dr. Harvey Gosser, Secretary-
Treasurer

AMERICAN ASSOCIATION OF
  VETERINARY PARASITOLOGISTS
  (AAVP)
Boehringer Ingelheim
Animal Health, Inc.
2621 N. Belt Highway
St. Joseph, MO 64506
Dr. Tom Kennedy, Executive
Secretary-Treasurer

AMERICAN BIRD CONSERVANCY
  (ABC)
1250 24th St., NW, Suite 400
Washington, DC 20037
George Fenwick, President
(202) 778-9666
FX (202) 778-9778
Email: *abc@abcbirds.org*
Web: *http://www.abcbirds.org*

AMERICAN BIRDING ASSOCIATION
  (ABA)
P.O. Box 6599
Colorado Springs, CO
80934-6599
Paul Gregen, Acting Executive
Director
(719) 578-1614
FX (719) 578-1480
Web: *http://www.americanbirding.
org*

AMERICAN BOARD OF VETERINARY
  PRACTITIONERS (ABVP)
530 Church Street, #700
Nashville, TN 37219-2321
Dr. Dee Ann Walker, CAE
(615) 254-7047

AMERICAN BUDGERIGAR SOCIETY
(ABS)
1600 W. Meadow Lane
Visalia, CA 93277
Linda Denny, Secretary
(209) 635-8903
Email: *absec@lightspeed.net*

AMERICAN COCKATIEL SOCIETY
(ACS)
9527 60th Lane North
Pinellas Park, FL 33782
(727) 541-4724
Email: *johnman@il.net*
Web: *http://www.asctiels.com*

AMERICAN COLLEGE OF
VETERINARY INTERNAL
MEDICINE (ACVIM)
1997 Wadsworth
Lakewood, CO 80215
June Pooley, Executive Director
(303) 231-9933
FX (303) 231-0880
Email: *acvim@acvim.org*
Web: *http://www.acvim.org*

AMERICAN COLLEGE OF
VETERINARY PATHOLOGISTS
(ACVP)
875 King Highway, Suite 200
Woodbury, NJ 08096-3172
Dr. Margaret Miller, Secretary-
Treasurer
(609) 848-7784

AMERICAN COLLEGE OF
VETERINARY SURGEONS (ACVS)
4340 East West Highway,
No. 401
Bethesda, MD 20814-4411
Dr. Ann Loew, Executive Director
(301) 718-6504
Email: *acvs@aol.com*
Web: *http://www.acvs.org*

AMERICAN FEDERATION OF
AVICULTURE (AFA)
P.O. Box 7312
N. Kansas City, MO 64116
(816) 421-BIRD (2473)
Web: *http://www.afa.birds.org*

AMERICAN HOLISTIC VETERINARY
MEDICAL ASSOCIATION
(AHVMA)
2214 Old Emmorton Road
Bel Air, MD 21015
Dr. Carvel G. Tiekert, Executive
Director
(410) 569-0795
Email: *74253.2560@compuserve.
com*

AMERICAN ORNITHOLOGISTS'
UNION (AOU)
Smithsonian Institute
Washington, DC 20560-0116
Ross Lein, Secretary
(202) 357-2051
FX (202) 633-8084
Email: *aou@nmnh.si.edu*

AMERICAN VETERINARY
CHIROPRACTIC ASSOCIATION
(AVCA)
623 Main Street
Hillsdale, IL 61257
Dr. Sharon L. Wildughby, Contact
(309) 658-2920

AMERICAN VETERINARY MEDICAL
ASSOCIATION (AVMA)
1931 N. Meacham Road
Suite 100
Schaumburg, IL 60173-4366
Dr. Bruce Little, Contact
(847) 925-8070
Web: *http://www.avma.org*

AMERICAN VETERINARY SOCIETY
FOR ANIMAL BEHAVIOR (AVSAB)
201 Cedarbrook Road
Naperville, IL 60565
Dr. Laurie Martin, Secretary-
Treasurer
FX: (630) 759-0094
Email: *martinala@juno.com*

ASSOCIATION OF FIELD
ORNITHOLOGISTS (AFO)
C/O Elissa Landre, President
Allen Press
P.O. Box 1897
Lawrence, KS 66044-1897

AVICULTURAL SOCIETY OF
AMERICA (ASA)
C/O Joe Krader, President
2910 Alps Road
Corona, CA 91719-3996

BIRD CLUBS OF AMERICA (BCA)
C/O Dick Ivy
P.O. Box 2005
Yorktown, VA 23692
(757) 898-5090

BIRDS OF NORTH AMERICA (BNA)
1900 Benjamin Franklin Parkway
Philadelphia, PA 19103-1101

BIRDS OF PREY REHABILITATION
FOUNDATION (BPRF)
2290 S. 104th Street
Broomfield, CO 80020
Sigrid Ueblacker, Executive
Officer
(303) 460-0674

THE COMPANION PARROT
QUARTERLY
P.O. Box 2428
Alameda, CA 94501
(510) 523-5303
Staff: @companionparrot.com
Web: *http://www.companionparrot.
com*

CORNELL LABORATORY OF
ORNITHOLOGY (CLO)
P.O. Box 11
Ithaca, NY 14851
John Fitzpatrick, Director
(607) 254-2425
FX (607) 254-2415
Web: *http://www.ornith.cornell.edu*

EASTERN BIRD BANDING
  ASSOCIATION (EBBA)
C/O Hannah B. Suthers,
Executive Officer
4 View Point Drive
Hopewell, NJ 08525
(609) 466-1871

HAWK MIGRATION ASSOCIATION
  OF NORTH AMERICA (HMANA)
P.O. Box 822
Boonton, NJ 07005-0822
William I. Gallagher, Secretary
(973) 335-0674
FX (973) 335-0674
Web: *http://www.hmana.org*

HAWK WATCH INTERNATIONAL
  (HWI)
1800 SW Temple, No. 226
Salt Lake City, UT 84115
Howard Gross, Director
(801) 484-6808
Email: *hwi@hawkwatch.org*
Web: *http://www.hawkwatch.org*

INLAND BIRD BANDING
  ASSOCIATION (IBBA)
150 U. Road
Wisner, NE 68791
(402) 529-6679

INTERNATIONAL ASSOCIATION OF
  AVIAN TRAINERS & EDUCATORS
  (IAATE)
2005 Victoria Road
St. Paul, MN 55118
FX (651) 994-9307
Web: *www.iaate.org*

INTERNATIONAL COMMITTEE ON
  VETERINARY ANATOMICAL
  NOMENCLATURE (ICVAN)
Department of Veterinary
Anatomy
Purdue University
West Lafayette, IN 47907-1242
Prof. R. L. Hullinger, Chairman
Email: *ronpat@laf.cioe.com*

INTERNATIONAL PARROTLET
  SOCIETY (IPS)
P.O. Box 2428
Santa Cruz, CA 95063
Sandee L. Molenda, Secretary
(831) 688-5560
FX (831) 689-9534
Email: *ips@parrotletranch.com*
Web: *http://www.parrotletranch.
com/ips*

INTERNATIONAL VETERINARY
  ACUPUNCTURE SOCIETY (IVAS)
268 W. 3rd Street, Suite 2
P.O. Box 2074
Nederland, CO 80466-2074
Dr. David H. Jaggar, Executive
Director
(303) 449-7936
Email: *ivasjagg@msn.com*
Web: *http://www.healthy.net*

Mid-Atlantic States
Association of Avian
Veterinarians (MASAAV)
Memorial Building, Suite 291
610 North Main Street
Blacksburg, VA 24060-3349
Keath L. Marx, DVM, Executive
Director
(540) 951-2559
FX (540) 953-0230
Email: *office@masaav.org*
Web: *http://www.masaav.org*

National Audubon Society
(NAS)
700 Broadway
New York, NY 10003
John B. Beinecke
(212) 979-3000
FX (212) 353-0377
Email: *webmaster@list.audubon.org*
Web: *http://www.audubon.org*

National Cockatiel Society
(NCS)
230 College Circle
Cedartown, GA 30125
Bill Rau, Membership & Bonds
Secretary
(919) 496-2649
Email: *brau@ipass.net*
Web: *http://www.cockatiels.org/ncs*

National Institute of Red
Orange Canaries and All
Other Caged Birds (NIROC)
1304 Fern Drive
Mount Prospect, IL 60056
Nancy Serchuk
(847) 437-4738
FX (847) 437-0413
Email: *gldnpkg@juno.com*

National Pigeon Association
(NPA)
C/O Pat Avery, Secretary-
Treasurer
P.O. Box 439
Newalla, OK 74857
(405) 386-6884
FX (405) 386-5541
Email: *james4bird@aol.com*
Web: *http://www.npausa@aol.com*

Society of Parrot Breeders &
Exhibitors (SPBE)
P.O. Box 369
Groton, MA 01450
Dr. Al E. Decoteau, Board
Chairman
(603) 672-4568
FX (603) 672-3120
Web: *http://www.spbe.org*

SOCIETY FOR NORTHWESTERN
  VERTEBRATE BIOLOGY (SNVB)
PMB 175
4820 Yelm Highway, Suite B
Olympia, WA 98503-4903
Janet Jones, Treasurer
(360) 753-7662
FX (360) 956-2346
Email: *ceeotters@aol.com*
Web: *http://www.eou.edu/snvb*

SOCIETY FOR THE PRESERVATION
  OF BIRDS OF PREY (SPBP)
12335 Santa Monica Boulevard
PMB 345
West Los Angeles, CA 90025
(310) 840-2322

VETERINARY CANCER SOCIETY
  (VCS)
2816 Monroe Avenue
Rochester, NY 14618
Dr. Robert Rosenthal,
Correspondence Secretary
(716) 271-5454

WORLD BIRD SANCTUARY (WBS)
P. O. Box 270270
St. Louis, MO 63127
Walter C. Crawford, Jr.,
Executive Director
(314) 938-6193
FX (314) 938-9464

Appendix B

Bird Bytes: Web Sites to Know*

AMERICAN COCKATIEL SOCIETY
http://www.acstiels.com/

AMERICAN FEDERATION OF
AVICULTURE
http://www.upatsix.com/afa/

AMERICAN HUMANE ASSOCIATION
http://www.americanhumane.org

AMERICAN SOCIETY FOR THE
PREVENTION OF CRUELTY TO
ANIMALS (ASPCA)
http://www.aspca.org

AN AMATEUR'S GUIDE FOR
KEEPING PARROTS
*http://www.geocities.com/
Heartland/4545/*

ANIMAL BIRD CONSERVANCY
http://www.abcbirds.org/

ANIMAL BIRDING ASSOCIATION
http://www.americanbirding.org/

ASSOCIATION OF AVIAN
VETERINARIANS
http://www.aav.org/

AUDUBON ON-LINE: NATIONAL
AUDUBON SOCIETY
http://www.audubon.org/

AVIAN & EXOTICS CLUB, UC
DAVIS SCHOOL OF VETERINARY
MEDICINE
*http://asucd.ucdavis.edu/
organizations/other/aemc/*

AVIAN RESOURCES OF SOUTHERN
CALIFORNIA
*http://home.earthlink.net/
~avianresourc/*

THE AVIARY
http://theaviary.com/

THE AVICULTURE SITE
*http://www.upatsix.com/other/
parrot.html*

AVITECH EXOTIC BIRDS
http://www.avitec.com/

BIG BIRD SEARCH — SEARCH
ENGINE
http://www.bigbirdsearch.com

* Alphabetically by name of Web site.

BIRD ASSOCIATIONS AND CLUBS
*http://www.e-alignet.com/
birdclub2.htm*

BIRD HEAVEN — MEMORIAL SITE
FOR PET BIRDS
*http://www.pet-
net.net/pet_birds/bird_heaven.htm*

BIRD LIFE ON-LINE
http://www.birdlife.com

BIRD LINKS TO THE WORLD
*http://www.ntic.qc.ca/~nellus/
links.html*

BIRD LOSS SYMPATHY CARDS
*http://www.fortunecity.com/
millennium/rainbow/339/
birdcards.html*

BIRD MYTHS BY NATIONAL PET
CLUB
*http://www.pet-
club.com/bird_myths.htm*

BIRD POEMS
*http://www.cybercomm.net/
~goldie/poems.html*

BIRD STUDIES AT CORNELL
UNIVERSITY
http://birds.cornell.edu/

BIRD TALK AVIAN LIBRARY
*http://www.animalnetwork.com/
birds/library/default.asp*

BIRD TALK MAGAZINE
*http://www.animalnetwork.com/
birds/default.asp*

BIRDS AND CHILDREN
*http://birding.about.com/hobbies/
birding/library/weekly/aa030798.htm*

BIRD HOTLINE
http://www.birdhotline.com/

BIRDS OF A FEATHER AVICULTURAL
SOCIETY
http://www.boaf.com/

BIRDS OF NORTH AMERICA
http://www.acnatsci.org/bna/

BIRD SOURCE
http://birdsource.cornell.edu/

CAGE BIRDS INDEX
*http://hometown.aol.com/
offmymedz/birds.html*

COMMUNICATION WITH PARROTS:
THE PEPPERBERG HOMEPAGE
*http://www.cages.org/research/
pepperberg/index.html*

THE COMPANION PARROT
QUARTERLY
http://www.companionparrot.com

THE COMPLETE BIRD PAGE
http://www.upatsix.com/

COOL BIRD POEMS
*http://www.usd.edu/~tgannon/
bird.html*

THE DELTA SOCIETY WEB SITE
*http://petsforum.com/deltasociety/
sitemap.htm*

THE DORIS DAY ANIMAL LEAGUE
(DDAL)
http://www.ddal.org

THE ECLECTUS SOCIETY
http://www.eclectus.com/

EXOTIC PET VET.NET
*http://www.exoticpetvet.net/
avianer.html*

FEATHER PLUCKING
http://www.featherpicking.com

FLOCKING SIMULATION
http://www.red3d.com/cwr/boids/

HUMANE SOCIETY OF THE UNITED
STATES
http://www.hsus.org/

THE INTERNATIONAL PARROTLET
SOCIETY
http://www.parrotletranch.com/ips/

LARRY'S FAMILY ANIMAL WEB SITE
http://www.familyanimal.com

LEARN BIRD SONGS WITH
BIRDWORKS
http://www.birdworksinc.com/

NATIONAL COCKATIEL SOCIETY
http://members.tripod.com/~ncs1/

NETVET
*http://www.netvet.wustl.edu/
vet.htm*

ON-LINE AUDIO FILES OF
BIRDSONGS
*http://algol.sirius.pisa.it/lipupisa/
snd/*

ON-LINE AVIAN RESOURCES
*http://members.tripod.com/
~raven86/aviary2.html*

THE ORNITHOLOGICAL WEB
LIBRARY
http://www.aves.net/the-owl/

ORNITHOLOGY WEB SITE
http://birdwebsite.com/

THE OWL PAGES
http://www.owlpages.com

PET BIRD REPORT
http://www.petbirdreport.com/

THE PET CHANNEL
http://www.thepetchannel.com

A PLACE FOR CANARIES
http://www.robirda.com

SOUTHEASTERN RAPTOR
REHABILITATION CENTER
*http://www.vetmed.auburn.edu/
raptor/*

SUNBIRD SEA COAST BIRD
SANCTUARY
http://webcoast.com/SeaBird/

TROPICAL BIRD FANCIERS
http://www.geocities.com/
heartland/5322/

THE VIRGINIA SOCIETY OF
ORNITHOLOGY
http://avery.med.virginia.edu/
~klk4p/vso/welcome.htm

Appendix C

Regional Bird Clubs in the United States*

CENTRAL ALABAMA AVICULTURAL
SOCIETY
Route 1, Box 412
Equality, AL 36026

ALASKA BIRD CLUB
Box 101825
Anchorage, AK 99510
(907) 345-0289

AVICULTURAL SOCIETY OF TUSCON
ARIZONA
P.O. Box 41501
Tucson, AZ 85717-1501

CAGE BIRD FANCIERS OF THE
OZARKS
Box 617
West Fork, AR 72774
(501) 839-2948

AVICULTURE SOCIETY OF AMERICA
Box 5516
Riverside, CA 92517

ROCKY MOUNTAIN SOCIETY OF
AVICULTURE
Box 3663
Englewood, CO 80155
(303) 369-4804

THE CONNECTICUT CANARY &
FINCH CLUB
P.O. Box 340145
Hartford, CT 06134

FLORIDA WEST COAST AVIAN
SOCIETY
Box 1905
Sarasota, FL 34230
(813) 966-6148

GEORGIA CAGE BIRD SOCIETY
3611 Whitfield Way
Powder Springs, GA 30073
(404) 439-1945

AVIAN RESEARCH ASSOCIATION
Chaminade University of
Honolulu
3140 Waialae Ave.
Honolulu, HI 96816

MAGIC VALLEY BIRD CLUB
2019 Sunrise Circle
Twin Falls, ID 83301
(208) 733-1455

* Alphabetically by State.

GREATER CHICAGO CAGE BIRD
CLUB
617 N. Meadows B. #2B
Addison, IL 60601
(708) 305-9043

INDIANA BIRD FANCIERS
2577 S. 775 East
Avilla, IN 46710

IOWA CAGE BIRD HOBBY CLUB
Box 37
Hudson, IA 50643
(319) 988-3087

KANSAS AVICULTURAL SOCIETY
455 S. Howe Rd.
Wichita, KS 67209
(316) 942-8864

CENTRAL KENTUCKY CAGE BIRD
SOCIETY
Box 24270
Lexington, KY 40524
(606) 273-8531

ARK-LA-TEX CAGE BIRD CLUB
6906 Buncombe Rd.
Shreveport, LA 71129
(318) 688-7863

MAINE STATE CAGED BIRD
SOCIETY
Box 5658
Augusta, ME 04322
(207) 677-2939

BALTIMORE BIRD FANCIERS
1114 Shady Dr.
Edgewood, MD 21040
(410) 538-5869

BOSTON COCKATIEL SOCIETY
93 Woodcliff Rd.
Chestnut Hill, MA 02167
(617) 286-4756

BOSTON SOCIETY FOR AVICULTURE
188 Highland St.
Boston, MA 02119
(617) 427-3773

GREAT LAKES AVICULTURAL
SOCIETY
Box 1293
Grand Rapids, MI 49501
(616) 534-7185

MINNESOTA COMPANION BIRD
ASSOCIATION
8090 Jensen Ave. S.
Cottage Grove, MN 55016
(612) 458-8698

MISSISSIPPI CAGE BIRD SOCIETY
Box 6683
Biloxi, MS 30530

MISSOURI CAGE BIRD
ASSOCIATION
2929 Indiana St.
St. Louis, MO 63118
(314) 664-8358

GREATER OMAHA CAGED BIRD
  SOCIETY
8018 Groves Circle
Omaha, NE 68147
(402) 733-8246

NEW HAMPSHIRE AVICULTURE
  SOCIETY
Box 575
Litteton, MA 01460
(603) 428-3628

CENTRAL JERSEY BIRD CLUB
1 Rex Court
Ringoes, NJ 08551
(908) 237-0557

LAS VEGAS AVICULTURAL SOCIETY
P.O. Box 270588
Las Vegas, NV 89127

NEW MEXICO BIRD CLUB
Box 90334
Albuquerque, NM 87199
(505) 823-1889

LONG ISLAND PARROT SOCIETY OF
  NY, INC.
P.O. Box 2754
North Babylon, NY 11703-0754

COASTAL CAROLINA BIRD SOCIETY
Harraden's Habitat
4315 Hwy. 70E
New Bern, NC 28562
(252) 637-5548

AVICULTURAL SOCIETY OF
  GREATER CINCINNATI
301 Ingram Rd.
Cincinnati, OH 45218
(513) 851-0912

OKLAHOMA AVICULTURAL SOCIETY
Box 691573
Tulsa, OK 74169
(912) 241-8831

RUFFLED FEATHERS BIRD CLUB
1403 E. First Ave.
Albany, OR 97321
(503) 926-7874

CENTRAL PENNSYLVANIA BIRD
  CLUB
19 Belview Rd.
Marysville, PA 17053
(717) 274-6713

RHODE ISLAND PET BIRD CLUB
Box 7190
Warwick, RI 02887

SOUTH CAROLINA BIRD BUDDIES
105 Eagle Nest Trail
West Columbia, SC 29169
(803) 796-1919

MINNESOTA PET BIRD SOCIETY
2001 N. Third Ave.
Sioux Falls, SD 57104
(605) 334-4891

GREATER MEMPHIS BIRD CLUB
371 Dreger
Memphis, TN 38109
(901) 332-7258

Fort Worth Bird Club
P.O. Box 7
Haslet, TX 76052

Aviculture Society of Utah
637 E. 900 S.
Salt Lake City, UT 84105
(801) 355-4408

Aviary Bird Club of Central
  Virginia
Rt. 2, Box 859
Forest, VA 24551

Northwest Exotic Bird Society
9594 First Ave. NE #352
Seattle, WA 98115

Wisconsin Cage Bird Club
505 McKinley
Omro, WI 54693
(414) 685-2242

Puerto Rico Canary Club
GPO Box 1704
San Juan, PR 00936

Bibliography, References and Suggested Reading

Alcock, John. (1998). *Animal Behavior: An Evolutionary Approach*. 6th Edition. Sinauer Associates, Inc., Publishers, Sunderland, Massachusetts.

Alderton, David. (1996). *101 Essential Tips: Caring for Your Pet Bird*. D.K. Publishing Company, New York.

Allport, Gordon W. (1958). *The Nature of Prejudice*. A Doubleday Anchor Book, New York.

Altman, Robert B., Ed. (1977). *Avian Medicine and Surgery*. W.B. Saunders Company, Orlando, Florida.

American Psychiatric Association. (1994). *Diagnostic and Statistical Manual of Mental Disorders, IV*. APA, Washington, D.C.

American Veterinary Medical Association. (1997). *U.S. Pet Ownership and Demographics Sourcebook*. Center for Information Management, Schaumburg, Illinois.

Armstrong, D. Stewart. (1998). *The Bird Care Handbook and Resource Guide*. Seacoast Publishing, Monterey, California.

Aronson, Elliot. Ed. (1999). *The Social Animal*. 8th Edition, Worth Publishers/W.H. Freeman & Company, New York.

Bailey, Covert. (1991). *The New Fit or Fat*. Houghton Mifflin Company, Boston.

Beck, Aaron T., M.D., and Emery, Gary, Ph.D. (1985). *Anxiety Disorders and Phobias: A Cognitive Perspective*. Basic Books, New York.

Beck, Aaron T., Rush, John A., Shaw, Brian F., and Emery, Gary. (1979). *Cognitive Therapy of Depression*. The Guilford Press, New York.

Boyle, W.A. (1999). *Sibling Rivalry, and Why Everyone (and Not Only Parents) Should Care About This Age-Old Problem*. Essay on the Web. URL: www.angelfire.com/md/imsystem/sibrivl.html

Brainerd, E.G., Jr., et. al. (1996). "Jealousy Induction as a Predictor of Power and the Use of Other Control Methods in Heterosexual Relationships." *Psychological Reports* 79, (2), 1319–25.

Buff, Sheila. Ed. (1991). *Flights of Fancy: A Treasury of Bird Quotations*. HarperCollins Publishers, New York.

Bibliography

Chatterjee, Sankar. (1997). *The Rise of Birds: 225 Million Years of Evolution.* Johns Hopkins University Press, Baltimore, Maryland.

Comer, Ronald J. (1999, 1996). *Fundamentals of Abnormal Psychology.* 2nd Edition, Worth Publishers/W.H. Freeman & Company, New York.

Cosgrove, Melba. (1976). *How to Survive the Loss of a Love.* Bantam Books, New York.

Doane, Bonnie Munro, and Qualkinbush, Thomas. (1994). *My Parrot, My Friend: An Owner's Guide to Parrot Behavior: Behavior Modification Techniques and Their Role in Contemporary Aviculture.* Howell Book House, New York.

Doane, Bonnie Munro. (1991). *The Parrot in Health and Illness.* Howell Book House, New York.

Doctor, Ronald M., Ph.D., and Kahn, Ada P. (1989). *The Encyclopedia of Phobias, Fears and Anxieties.* Facts On File, Inc., New York.

Dolan, M., and Bishay, N. (1996). "The Effectiveness of Cognitive Therapy in the Treatment of Non-Psychotic Morbid Jealousy." *British Journal of Psychiatry.* 168 (5), 588–93.

Feduccia, Alan. (1996). *The Origin and Evolution of Birds.* Yale University Press, New Haven, Connecticut.

Ferrari, Michael. (1986). "Fears and Phobias in Childhood." *Child Psychiatry and Human Development,* Volume 17, p. 75.

Gibbons, Paul, and Horton, Susan J. (2000). *Journal of Avian Medicine & Surgery.* 14(1): 60–64, March.

Gibran, Kahlil. (1978). *The Prophet.* Alfred A. Knopf, New York.

Grindol, Diane. (1998). *The Complete Book of Cockatiels.* Howell Book House, New York.

Hall, Calvin S., and Lindzey, Gardner. (1978). *Theories of Personality.* 3rd Edition. John Wiley & Sons, New York.

Kay, William. (1995). *Pet Loss and Human Bereavement.* Iowa State University Press, Iowa.

Keirsey, David. (1978). *Please Understand Me.* Prometheus Nemesis Books Company, California.

Kübler-Ross, Elisabeth. (1969). *On Death and Dying.* Macmillan Publishing, New York.

Lachman, Larry & Mickadeit, Frank. (2000). *Cats on the Counter: Therapy and Training for Your Cat.* St. Martin's Press, New York.

Lachman, Larry, and Mickadeit, Frank. (1999). *Dogs on the Couch: Behavior Therapy for Training and Caring for Your Dog.* The Overlook Press, New York.

Lassen, Maureen K., and McConnell, Stephen C. (1977). "Treatment of a Severe Bird Phobia by Participant Modeling." *Journal of Behavior Therapy & Experimental Psychiatry.* 8 (2): 165–68.

Leman, Kevin. (1998, 1985). *The Birth Order Book: Why You Are the Way You Are.* Fleming H. Revell, Grand Rapids, Michigan.

Levine, Bettijane. (1999). "Grief Is OK When You Lose a Pet." *Los Angeles Times.* May 3, p. E-2.

Levy, Naomi. (1998). *To Begin Again: The Journey Toward Comfort, Strength, and Faith in Difficult Times.* Alfred A. Knopf, New York.

Minuchin, Salvador. (1974). *Families and Family Therapy.* Harvard University Press, Cambridge, Massachusetts.

Murphy, Edward F. (1996). *2,715 One-Line Quotations, for Speakers, Writers & Raconteurs.* Gramercy Books, New York.

Partington, Angela. Ed. (1997, 1993). *The Concise Oxford Dictionary of Quotations.* Oxford University Press, Oxford and New York.

Pepperberg, Irene Maxine. (1999). *The Alex Studies: Cognitive and Communicative Abilities of Grey Parrots.* Harvard University Press, Cambridge, Massachusetts, and London, England.

Ponterotto, Joseph G., and Pedersen, Paul B. (1993). *Preventing Prejudice: A Guide for Counselors and Educators.* Sage Publications, Newbury Park, California.

Quackenbush, Jamie. (1985). *When Your Pet Dies: How to Cope with Your Feelings.* Simon & Schuster, New York.

Rachman, S. (1990). "The Determinants and Treatment of Simple Phobias." *Advances in Behavior Research and Therapy,* Volume 13, pp. 1–30.

Rando, Therese A. (1991, 1988). *How to Go On Living When Someone You Love Dies.* Bantam Books, New York.

Rosenman, Martin F. (1979). *Loving Styles: A Guide For Increasing Intimacy.* Prentice-Hall, Inc., Englewood Cliffs, New Jersey.

Roth, Geneen. (1989). *When Food Is Love: Exploring the Relationship Between Eating and Intimacy.* Plume, Penguin Group, New York.

Ryan, Thomas, D.V.M. (1989). *Companion Animal Practice.* 12 (8), 31–32.

Sanders, Catherine M. (1992). *Surviving Grief and Learning to Live Again.* John Wiley & Sons, Inc., New York.

Schneidman, Edwin. (1980). *Voices of Death.* Harper & Row, New York.

Scott, D.L. (1970). "Treatment of a Severe Phobia for Birds by Hypnosis." *American Journal of Clinical Hypnosis.* 12 (3), 146–49.

Sheats, Cliff. (1992, 1995). *Lean Bodies: The Revolutionary New Approach to Losing Bodyfat by Increasing Calories.* Warner Books, New York.

The Princeton Language Institute. (1993). *21st Century Dictionary of Quotations.* Dell Publishing, New York.

Todd, Frank S., Ed. (1994). *10,001 Titillating Tidbits of Avian Trivia.* Ibis Publishing Company, Vista, California.

Sdorow, Lester M. (1993). *Psychology.* WCB Brown & Benchmark Publishers, Dubuque, Iowa.

Stunkard, Jim, D.V.M. (1984). *Diagnosis and Treatment and Husbandry of Pet Birds.* 2nd Edition. Stunkard Publishing Company, Edgewater, Maryland.

Walker, G.B.R. (1993). *Colored, Type & Song Canaries.* Seacoast Publishing, Monterey, California.

Wolpe, Joseph, M.D. (1982). *The Practice of Behavior Therapy.* 3rd Edition, Pergamon Press, New York.

Worden, J. William. (1991). *Grief Counseling and Grief Therapy: A Handbook for the Mental Health Practitioner.* Springer Publishing Company, New York.

Wrightsman, Lawrence S. (2001). *Forensic Psychology.* Wadsworth/Thomson Learning, Belmont, California.

Index